Work Practice & Experience

LEVELS 5 & 6

D1495186

Work Practice & Experience in Childcare

LEVELS **5 & 6**

Martina Coombes and Joanne Russell

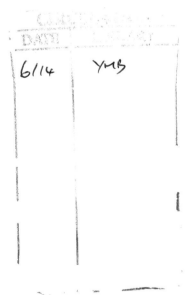
Gill & Macmillan

Gill & Macmillan
Hume Avenue
Park West
Dublin 12
with associated companies throughout the world
www.gillmacmillan.ie

©Martina Coombes and Joanne Russell 2014

978 07171 5978 9

Print origination by O'K Graphic Design, Dublin
Printed by GraphyCems, Spain

For permission to reproduce photographs, the authors and publisher gratefully acknowledge the
following:

© Alamy: 27, 28, 118; © Blogger: 144; © Department of Social Protection: 96; © Equality Authority: 38;
© Facebook: 143; © Google: 145T; © Health and Safety Authority: 30; © HootSuite: 145B; © ICTU: 40T;
© LinkedIn: 139; © NQAI: 129; © Rex Features: 25; © Shutterstock: 26, 32, 34, 36, 39, 40B, 44, 46, 48;
© Twitter: 142; Courtesy of An Garda Síochána: 78.

The paper used in this book comes from the wood pulp of managed forests. For every tree felled, at least
one tree is planted, thereby renewing natural resources.

A CIP catalogue record is available for this book from the British Library

Contents

CHAPTER ONE

Working in the Early Childhood Care and Education Sector

In this chapter

- Work organisations: types (public, private and the voluntary sector), structures and roles
- Personal work/career opportunities in the early childhood care and education (ECCE), education and social care sectors
- Childcare qualifications
- Síolta's principles and links to practice
- Aistear's themes and links to practice

BACKGROUND

It is useful for those working in early childhood care and education (ECCE) to have some knowledge of the historical context of the childcare sector to enable them to understand the context of childcare provision today.

Private, public and voluntary childcare services

Childcare services in Ireland have historically been provided by the private profit-making sector. The introduction of the ECCE scheme in January 2010 was very important as it provided universal provision of childcare placements for children in playschool. The ECCE scheme provides a one-year placement for pre-school children and is not means tested. Services in the childcare sector are mainly provided by private ECCE services that are operated as a business, and this affects the costing, budgeting and resource allocations in an early childhood service.

The state does provide some public childcare services, including early intervention programmes such as Early Start, HighScope and community pre-schools and crèches. These, however, represent a very small component of service provision in Ireland and are not available in all areas of the country.

Do some research to find out more about Early Start, HighScope and community crèches.

In the past, childcare in Ireland was usually provided by family members or by childminders. Today families and childminders are still significant providers of childcare services in Ireland, along with crèches, sessional services, naíonraí, after-school facilities and specialised services such as the Forest Schools (outdoor playschools). Public funding for childcare is extremely limited and is primarily oriented towards the development of childcare facilities in designated geographical areas of disadvantage.

Households with lower incomes rely on publicly subsidised childcare, which is limited and, depending on where they live, may not be available. Middle- and higher-income families pay high costs in the private marketplace. Public provision for pre-school childcare is only available to a very small proportion of pre-school children – around 4% of the total number of children accessing childcare in Ireland.

DIFFERENT TYPES OF CHILDCARE SERVICE

There are a number of different services currently provided in Ireland today in the ECCE sector. They include the following.

Full day care

This is a structured care service where children attend for more than 3.5 hours per day. Providers typically care for children from 3 months to 6 years. Some services may also include an after-school facility, typically for children from 4 to 12 years of age. In full day care, sleeping arrangements and food preparation must meet standards laid down by the Health Service Executive (HSE) and the Child Care (Pre-School Services) Regulations 2006. Providers include day nurseries and crèches.

Sessional services

Sessional services provide planned programmes of up to 3.5 hours per session (such as a morning or an afternoon). In general these sessions cater for children between 2.5 years and 6 years of age, but they can also be provided for younger children. In order to provide a sessional childcare service, a recognised childcare qualification is required by staff working in the service. Sessional services include:

▶ **Montessori groups:** focus on individualised education, teaching social skills and maximising children's development. They cater to children up to the age of 6 in an ECCE setting.

▶ **Parent and toddler groups:** a group of parents, guardians or carers and children come together for supervised play and companionship for their parents.

▶ **Naíonraí:** nursery schools or playschools operating through the medium of Irish.
▶ **Playschools:** give children an opportunity to play with other children of a similar age, learn to share and take turns and to understand the rules of the classroom, such as listening.

The curricula offered in ECCE services include Froebel, Steiner Waldorf, HighScope, Reggio Emilia and Forest Schools. (These can all be explored in the Early Childhood Award FETAC Level 5 or Early Childhood Curriculum FETAC Level 6, awarded by QQI.)

Childminders

Childminders care for children in the minder's own home or in the child's home. A childminder can care for up to five children under 6 years of age (including the childminder's own child or children). The service is usually offered for a full working day or for different periods during the day. Parents and childminders arrange their own terms and conditions.

Advantages
▶ The child is typically one of a small group, which should mean more one-to-one attention.
▶ The childminder can look after children of different ages, which replicates a family situation.
▶ Childminders often look after children from when they are very young until they go to secondary school. This allows the child to build a relationship with the childminder and provides the child with security and consistency of care.
▶ Taking your child to a childminder can be a very good substitute for home care. The childminder may even be located near to the family home or may work in the child's or children's own home.
▶ Typically, childminders are more flexible about pick-up and drop-off times.

Disadvantages
▶ There may not be a back-up childcare service for when the childminder is sick or on holiday.
▶ A childminder does not need to register, so they are unregulated and may not have any specific childcare training.
▶ A childminder may pay more attention to their own children than to the other children in their care.

Au pairs

An au pair is typically a young person who is treated as a family member in exchange for certain services, such as light housework or helping to mind the children. It is a voluntary arrangement between a private household and a private individual. The objective of the arrangement is to enable the au pair to experience a different culture and improve his or her foreign language skills.

There is no specific regulatory framework, and au pairs are not required to have any specific experience of working with children. An au pair is not a professional nanny or childminder. Au pairs are not employees and there is no contract of employment between the host family and the au pair. The au pair is usually given room and board and paid a small weekly allowance. There are specialist private agencies that arrange the placement of au pairs with families.

Drop-in centres

A drop-in centre offers a service for short periods during the day. These centres are often provided in shopping centres, leisure centres, community halls and accommodation facilities, etc. The service is provided as part of a customer or client service and children are looked after while the parent is availing of a service or attending an event. This provision is typically time limited.

School-age childcare

Services for schoolchildren can include breakfast clubs in schools, after-school clubs and school holiday programmes such as summer camps, etc. Some school-age childcare is privately provided and is one of a number of services offered by a childcare service. Depending on the service, there may also be homework supervision, planned activities or a nutritious meal. Children aged from 4 to 12 years are catered for. There are currently no specific regulations in relation to adult/child ratios or programme delivery in an after-school service.

Affordable childcare

Affordable childcare is provided for families on lower incomes, and also to support parents to return to work or education. This type of service is called a community childcare facility. Funding is available through the National Childcare Investment Programme. The local City/County Childcare Committee will provide information on affordable childcare services.

Information about the National Childcare Investment Programme can be found on the Pobal website (www.pobal.ie) under 'Funding Programmes'.

Special needs assistants

Special needs assistants (SNAs) support children with special needs, typically in a mainstream school but sometimes in an ECCE setting or a special school. The role of the SNA is to assist with the individual needs of a child who presents with a physical, intellectual or emotional disability or a combination of these. The SNA is appointed by the school to support a child/children in the classroom and the allocation of SNA support may be made on a full- or part-time basis.

The duties of an SNA

The duties of SNAs are outlined in Appendix 1 of Circular DES SP.ED 07/02. An SNA's role is a non-teaching role. A student with a general learning disability would not typically require the services of an SNA.

In accordance with Circular 10/76: Duties and Responsibilities of Principal Teachers, the duties of SNAs are assigned by the principal teacher and sanctioned by the board of management. Their work should be supervised either by the principal or by a class teacher.

Those duties involve tasks of a non-teaching nature, such as:

- preparing and tidying classroom(s) in which the pupil(s) with special needs is/are being taught
- assisting children to board and alight from school buses; where necessary, travel as escort on school buses may be required
- special assistance as necessary for pupils with particular difficulties, e.g. helping physically disabled pupils with typing or writing
- assistance with clothing, feeding, toileting and general hygiene
- assisting on out-of-school visits, walks and similar activities
- assisting teachers in the supervision of pupils with special needs during assembly, recreational and dispersal periods
- accompanying individuals or small groups who may have to be withdrawn temporarily from the classroom
- general assistance to the class teachers, under the direction of the principal, with duties of a non-teaching nature (SNAs may not act as substitute or temporary teachers; in no circumstances may they be left in sole charge of a class).

Where an SNA has been appointed to assist a school in catering for a specific pupil, duties should be modified to support the particular needs of the pupil concerned. (See www.education.ie, accessed 31 October 2013.)

Qualifications

The qualifications for an SNA, as laid down by the Department of Education and Skills, are (as at October 2013): a FETAC Level 3 (awarded by QQI) major qualification on the National Framework of Qualifications; or a minimum of three grade Ds in the Junior Certificate; or equivalent.

It is important to note, however, that although these are the basic qualifications, many schools require higher qualifications, such as a FETAC Level 5 or 6 childcare award that incorporates the Special Needs modules at these levels.

Social care work

Work in social care typically involves working with marginalised or disadvantaged people and communities in a caring, compassionate way. Social care work includes working with: children and adolescents in residential child care; children/adults with learning disabilities; homeless people; people with alcohol/drug dependency; families in the community; elderly people; and asylum seekers/refugees. Typically the qualification needed to be a social care worker is a Level 7 degree in social care or equivalent. These degrees are offered at colleges and universities, including institutes of technology, throughout Ireland.

Students who have completed a FETAC award in childcare sometimes decide that they would like to work in social care and apply using their FETAC qualifications or as a mature student for entry to the social care degree programme.

NATIONAL CHILDCARE STRATEGY 2006–2010

As part of the National Childcare Strategy 2006–2010, the National Childcare Investment Programme provides for the quantity and quality of childcare facilities in Ireland. It is also responsible for co-ordinating childcare activities from national to local level.

Community Childcare Subvention Programme

The purpose of this programme is to support community-based childcare services and to facilitate them in providing quality childcare services at reduced rates to disadvantaged parents.

The Childcare Directorate at the Department of Children and Youth Affairs has responsibility for implementing the National Childcare Strategy 2006–2010. Its Guide for Parents is available at www.omc.gov.ie/documents/childcare/childcare_parents.pdf.

City/County Childcare Committees

The City/County Childcare Committees (CCCs) develop and implement a co-ordinated strategy for the provision of quality, affordable and accessible childcare in each county. The CCCs help communities identify gaps in current childcare services and develop new services to meet these needs. They provide information on funding and grant applications and facilitate a co-ordinated approach to childcare training at all levels. The available grants change from time to time, but at the time of writing there are grants available for the development of community services.

Childcare costs depend on the type of childcare service that is chosen, the number of hours and the level of staff training in that facility.

CHILDCARE QUALIFICATIONS

▶ **The Child Care (Pre-School Services) Regulations 2006** require that a minimum of 50% of staff in a service have a qualification appropriate to the care and development of children.

▶ **The Early Childhood Care and Education Scheme** states that from June 2012 the play leader in each room of a service must have a minimum qualification of a FETAC Level 5 Certificate in Childcare.

▶ **Employers** generally look for a minimum of FETAC Level 5 award in Early Childhood Care and Education or an equivalent qualification relevant to the specific job role and responsibilities.

▶ **The ECCE scheme** pays a higher rate per child (€75 at the time of writing) if the childcare leader has a degree in Early Childhood Education at Level 7 or above.

SÍOLTA

Síolta is the national quality framework for ECCE in Ireland. It provides the framework for evaluating the quality of service provision in an ECCE service. Síolta comprises three distinct but interrelated elements: Principles, Standards and Components of Quality.

The elements of Síolta

Principles

Standards

Components of Quality

Síolta's 12 Principles provide the overall ethos of the framework, and there are also 16 Quality Standards and 75 Components that all ECCE services are required to work towards. It details core principles to which all services must adhere and guides service providers and practitioners towards quality practice in all areas of service provision. Síolta is also a self-assessment Quality Assurance Programme.

First published in 2006, Síolta was developed by the Centre for Early Childhood Development and Education (CECDE), on behalf of the then Department of Education and Science. The word Síolta means 'seeds' in Irish, and the symbol of the seed is used as a means of communicating the ways in which the framework can be used as a developmental tool, enabling the development of each service to its full potential and in its own unique way.

Síolta is designed to improve the quality of all elements of practice in an ECCE setting where children from the ages of 0 to 6 years attend. These settings include:

▶ full-time and part-time day care settings
▶ childminders
▶ pre-school sessional services
▶ primary school infant classes.

You should consider the Síolta Principles in your work practice and see how they are applied in your work placement.

Access Síolta's Principles at www.siolta.ie/principles.php.

Principle 1

Early childhood is a significant and distinct time in life that must be nurtured, respected, valued and supported in its own right.

Early childhood, the period from birth to six years, is a significant and unique time in the life of every individual. Every child needs and has the right to positive experiences in early childhood. As with every other phase in life, positive supports and adequate resources are necessary to make the most of this period. Provision of such supports and resources should not be conditional on the expectations of the economy, society or other interests.

In practice

Consider how this principle can be applied in your work placement practice. How do you promote positive experiences for the children you work with? Are the necessary resources available in the ECCE setting you are working in? What are the necessary supports and resources needed? Consider what economic/societal factors might affect provision of services. How could you convince a service manager that more supports and resources are needed to satisfy this principle?

Principle 2

The child's individuality, strengths, rights and needs are central in the provision of quality early childhood experiences.

The child is an active agent in her/his own development through her/his interactions with the world. These interactions are motivated by the individual child's abilities, interests, previous experiences and desire for independence. Each child is a competent learner from birth and quality early years experiences can support each child to realise their full potential. Provision of these experiences must reflect and support the child's strengths, needs and interests. Children have the right to be listened to and have their views on issues that affect them heard, valued and responded to.

In practice

Do you take the time to get to know the children you work with? Do you know their likes and dislikes? How do you promote their independence? Do you scaffold their learning? How is the child supported to achieve their full potential? Do you listen to the children you are working with; and how do you demonstrate that you have heard them? Were there times when you did not listened to the child/children? What were the consequences of this? What do you do when you do not know how to support the child/children in your care? Who checks that children are provided with learning experiences suited to their needs?

Principle 3

Parents are the primary educators of the child and have a pre-eminent role in promoting her/his well-being, learning and development.

Quality early childhood care and education must value and support the role of parents. Open, honest and respectful partnership with parents is essential in promoting the best interests of the child. Mutual partnership contributes to establishing harmony and continuity between the diverse environments the child experiences in the early years. The development of connections and interactions between the early childhood setting, parents, the extended family and the wider community also adds to the enrichment of early childhood experiences by reflecting the environment in which the child lives and grows.

In practice

Consider the communication channels and methods used in your work placement setting. Are they included in curriculum planning? Do you have a parents' noticeboard? Does the provider have a website and/or Facebook page? Are communication books sent home with each child? Are notices printed and sent home in the children's bags? Why do you think this is the case? Are parents truly involved in their children's learning and development in the ECCE setting? Are parents given the opportunity to evaluate the services provided? How is parent-to-service communication recorded? How is service-to-parent communication recorded?

Principle 4

Responsive, sensitive and reciprocal relationships, which are consistent over time, are essential to the well-being, learning and development of the young child.

The relationships that the child forms within her/his immediate and extended environment from birth will significantly influence her/his well-being, development and learning. These relationships are two way and include adults, peers, family and the extended community. Positive relationships, which are secure, responsive and respectful and which provide consistency and continuity over time, are the cornerstone of the child's well-being.

In practice

How do you ensure relationship building and bonding with the children you work with in your ECCE setting? Why is key working important? How does it promote bonding in an early years setting? How do you role-model behaviour? Is there anything in your behaviour that needs to change to support the well-being of the children in the service? What do you do when a relationship breaks down in the workplace? How does a relationship breakdown affect your practice? Have you received in-house training on how to communicate with stakeholders?

Principle 5

Equality is an essential characteristic of quality early childhood care and education.

Equality, as articulated in Article 2 of the UN Convention on the Rights of the Child (1989) and in the Equal Status Acts 2000 to 2004, is a fundamental characteristic of quality early childhood care and education provision. It is a critical prerequisite for supporting the optimal development of all children in Ireland. It requires that the individual needs and abilities of each child are recognised and supported from birth towards the realisation of her/his unique potential. This means that all children should be able to gain access to, participate in, and benefit from early years services on an equal basis.

In practice

How is equality of opportunity promoted in your ECCE service? Why is equality of opportunity different from equality of treatment? How does the curriculum and planning promote the optimal development of children, enabling them to reach their full potential? What would you do if you witnessed practices that run counter to equality legislation? Do you truly value equality?

Principle 6

Quality early childhood settings acknowledge and respect diversity and ensure that all children and families have their individual, personal, cultural and linguistic identity validated.

Diversity is a term which is generally used to describe differences in individuals by virtue of gender, age, skin colour, language, sexual orientation, ethnicity, ability, religion, race or other background factors such as family structure and economic circumstances. Quality early childhood environments should demonstrate respect for diversity through promoting a sense of belonging for all children within the cultural heritage of Ireland. They should also provide rich and varied experiences which will support children's ability to value social and cultural diversity.

In practice

In your placement, are all the children you work with represented? How are they represented? Do the books, toys, posters, art, language used and cultural events and activities all reflect the diversity of the children you work with? If you cannot source material to ensure diversity, how could you overcome this? How will you deal with parents who are concerned with diversity?

Note: links with Aistear – Identity and Belonging – are important here.

Principle 7

The physical environment of the young child has a direct impact on her/his well-being, learning and development.

The child's experiences in early childhood are positively enhanced by interactions with a broad range of environments. These include the indoor and outdoor, built and natural, home and out-of-home environments. The environment should be high quality and should extend and enrich the child's development and learning. These experiences stimulate curiosity, foster independence and promote a sense of belonging. The development of respect for the environment will also result from such experiences.

In practice

Do the children you work with have access to an outdoor play area? The weather is seldom bad enough to prevent outdoor play: when the outdoors is neglected it is more often because of inappropriate clothing or staff who are reluctant to go outside when it is cold or wet. How does the ECCE setting promote the children's development? How does the physical environment support the child's learning? Examine the room/

rooms you are working in: is there a home corner, construction area, creative section, water/sand play area, dress up/role play/book corner, etc.? How does each of these areas promote the child's learning and development? How is each play area physically defined, i.e. in the layout of the room(s)?

Principle 8

The safety, welfare and well-being of all children must be protected and promoted in all early childhood environments.

The promotion of child well-being is a characteristic of a quality environment. This involves the protection of each child from harmful experiences and the promotion of child welfare. Additionally, the opportunity to form trusting relationships with adults and other children is a key characteristic of quality. Promotion of safety should not prevent the child from having a rich and varied array of experiences in line with her/his age and stage of development.

In practice

Health and safety are important considerations in any childcare or work environment. Drawing up a safety statement (see Chapter 3) helps to identify potential risks and to develop work practices and/or policies to minimise or reduce risk. Activities and play can be risk assessed and developing an understanding of health and safety should not prohibit a child from the 'dignity of risk' in developing and engaging in activities that are age- and stage-appropriate. Conduct your own risk assessment of the room you work in, and of a planned activity. What recommendations, if any, could you make?

Principle 9

The role of the adult in providing quality early childhood experiences is fundamental.

Quality early childhood practice is built upon the unique role of the adult. The competencies, qualifications, dispositions and experience of adults, in addition to their capacity to reflect upon their role, are essential in supporting and ensuring quality experiences for each child. This demanding and central role in the life of the young child needs to be appropriately resourced, supported and valued.

In practice

Professionally qualified staff are important in an ECCE setting. The HSE requires that at least 50% of all staff in an ECCE service should have a FETAC Level 5 award in childcare. The ability of the childcare practitioner to reflect on their practice and to develop new and better ways of working with children is an important competency to develop. What opportunities for reflection are you provided with in the workplace?

Principle 10

The provision of quality early childhood experiences requires cooperation, communication and mutual respect.

Teamwork is a vital component of quality in early childhood care and education. It is the expression of cooperative, coordinated practice in any setting. Shared knowledge and understanding, clearly communicated among the team within the setting; with and among other professionals involved with the child; and with the parents is a prerequisite of quality practice and reflects a 'whole-child perspective'. This also ensures the promotion of respectful working relationships among all adults supporting the well-being, learning and development of the child. Such teamwork, coordination and communication must be valued, supported and resourced by an appropriate infrastructure at local, regional and national levels.

In practice

Being able to work as part of a team is very important in an ECCE setting. The team includes not only your colleagues but also the children you work with, their parents and the wider community. Communication, both verbal and non-verbal, is a very important component of team working. Active listening also promotes a respectful working relationship. A childcare service should aim to facilitate effective communication and teamwork. What policies are in place to ensure a respectful working environment? What happens when conflict arises? (Communication is dealt with in Chapter 8.)

Principle 11

Pedagogy in early childhood is expressed by curricula or programmes of activities which take a holistic approach to the development and learning of the child and reflect the inseparable nature of care and education.

Pedagogy is a term that is used to refer to the whole range of interactions which support the child's development. It takes a holistic approach by embracing both care and education. It acknowledges the wide range of relationships and experiences within which development takes place and recognises the connections between them. It also supports the concept of the child as an active learner. Such pedagogy must be supported within a flexible and dynamic framework that addresses the learning potential of the 'whole child'. Furthermore, it requires that early childhood practitioners are adequately prepared and supported for its implementation.

In practice

The interactions in an ECCE setting should promote the child's learning and development. The child should be an active participant in their learning, not a passive recipient of information. A child's care and education are supported in an ECCE setting. The holistic development of the child needs to be supported and this includes the child's social, emotional, cognitive, language, physical, moral and spiritual development. Over a period of time, consider the holistic development of children in your placement. Are all these elements in the pedagogical framework implemented in your placement? Is there any bias towards one element? Consider how to integrate numerous elements into one activity – can all elements be drawn together?

Principle 12

Play is central to the well-being, development and learning of the young child.

Play is an important medium through which the child interacts with, explores and makes sense of the world around her/him. These interactions with, for example, other children, adults, materials, events and ideas, are key to the child's well-being, development and learning. Play is a source of joy and fulfilment for the child. It provides an important context and opportunity to enhance and optimise quality early childhood experiences. As such, play will be a primary focus in quality early childhood settings.

> **In practice**
>
> The stages of play should be supported in an ECCE setting. Different types of play should be evident, including creative play, construction play, role play, heuristic play and so on. The curriculum in the ECCE setting should reflect play as the conduit to enabling the child to learn and develop to their full potential. Play should be fun. How do you ensure that all children enjoy activities? How do you encourage shy children to play as part of a group activity? What are the challenges you have experienced when designing play activities? What do you reflect on when observing children playing? How do you handle observations that worry you, for example potential bullying behaviour, concerns about racism, etc.? Consider your behaviour during play activities. Are you involved? Should you be more actively involved?

Síolta is used in conjunction with the Aistear curriculum framework.

AISTEAR

In this section, we present an overview of Aistear as a curriculum framework, we evaluate it and look at how it can be used in an ECCE setting.

Aistear, the early childhood curriculum framework, celebrates childhood as a time of being, of enjoying learning from experiences as they unfold. It provides information for adults who work in an ECCE/school setting to help them plan for and provide enjoyable and challenging learning experiences, so that the children who have access to this curriculum can grow and develop into competent learners who have loving relationships with others. Aistear informs practice across a range of settings, disciplines and professions, and it encourages interdisciplinary work. One of the key elements of Aistear is that it can be used in conjunction with other approaches such as Montessori, Steiner, HighScope and other curricula.

Aistear complements and extends existing curriculum and materials, identifying what and how children should learn and describing the types of experience that support learning. It makes connections in children's learning through the early childhood years as they move from one setting to another; supports parents as their children's primary educators during early childhood; and promotes effective partnerships between parents and practitioners. The Aistear curriculum framework identifies important themes that permeate ECCE.

Aistear's Themes

Well-being

Identity and Belonging

Communicating

Exploring and Thinking

1   **Well-being:** children should be confident, happy and healthy.

2   **Identity and belonging:** children develop a positive sense of who they are, and feel that they are valued and respected as part of a family and community.

3   **Communicating:** children share their experiences, thoughts, ideas and feelings with others with growing confidence and competence in a variety of ways and for a variety of purposes.

4   **Exploring and thinking:** children are enabled to make sense of things, people and places in their world by interacting with others; by playing, observing, investigating, questioning, forming, testing and refining ideas.

It is very difficult to evaluate the Aistear curriculum as it is not a universal provision in the ECCE sector; it is a model that can be incorporated into other curriculum methodologies.

There is a requirement for all services that participate in the ECCE scheme to adhere to the quality assurance model of Síolta, but at the time of writing there is no requirement to implement Aistear. However, the Local Childcare Committees, which were established in 2001 by the Minister for Children, and of which there are 34 countrywide, are very much invested in the Aistear curriculum and provide training in Aistear for ECCE providers.

HOW WORK EXPERIENCE RELATES TO PRACTICE

We have so far looked at different childcare providers, national strategies that affect childcare services and curricula that inform the daily education and care of pre-school children. We must now consider how the other modules/courses that you are studying also impact on your learning and development as a childcare practitioner. The following are examples of what you may have learned or are learning in your childcare courses that you can apply to your practice in an ECCE setting.

Observation

▶ Examine how to use your observation theory when working with children. For example, identify what they like to do, and which toys/equipment they choose during free play.

▶ Are there any boy/girl differences in the activities they prefer? What gender theories have you learned? What role does Bandura's social learning theory have in relation to gender identities?

▶ Why is this information important?

▶ What do you know about the difference time of day makes for children? Are there different moods evident throughout the day? Are the children different in the morning and the afternoon? Does the day of the week make a difference?

(Adapted from Flood (2013))

Health and safety

▶ What have you learned about health and safety, fire drills, cleaning routines, illnesses, lifting and first aid? Are you familiar with the Safety, Health and Welfare at Work Act 2005?

▶ Consider what you know about all of these and why they will be important in your ECCE work placement setting.

▶ Is a tidy-up routine for the children important? If so, why would this be so? Consider ways you could encourage the children to help.

(For further information, see Kinsella (2012))

Children's routines

▶ Why do you need to understand the routine of the children you will work with?

▶ Why do we need to consider if they have settled in well? Or if they know what happens next in their daily routine?

▶ Why is consistency important in an ECCE setting and what will you do to ensure consistency in your practice?

Understanding the needs of different age groups

▶ What are the needs of the different age groups – babies, wobblers, toddlers and pre-school children – with whom you will be working in your work placement?

▶ Think about the work of cognitive theorist such as Piaget and social development theorist such as Vygotsky when considering how to meet a child's individual needs.

Greeting children and their families

▶ What have you learned about meeting and greeting children and their families when they come to the ECCE setting?

▶ How can you help a child who is upset when they arrive at the ECCE setting?

Behaviour management

▶ What have you learned about behaviour management?

▶ How will you apply what you have learned about behaviour management in your work placement? Think about the role of positive reinforcement and operant conditioning. Refer to the ECCE setting's policies and procedure on behaviour management.

Children whose first language is not English

▶ What do you need to consider in your work placement if working with a child or children whose first language is not English?

▶ Why do you need to take note of the range of language abilities in the setting?

▶ Should you compare the understanding and type of language used by the different children? What about the children who are only children or those who come from larger families? Describe the different approaches needed to deal with each of these children.

Play

▶ What do you need to know about the different types of play children engage in? When the children go outside to play, is there a difference between what boys like to do and what girls like to do?

▶ What do we understand about solitary play, parallel play and co-operative play?

▶ What should the adult carers do while the children are outdoors? Have you prepared some activities for the children to do before you start your placement?

Policies and procedures

▶   What do you know about your service? Do you need to familiarise yourself with the service/school prior to or during your placement?

▶   What are the purpose of policies and procedures in an ECCE setting? What do you already know about policies and procedures?

Background information on children/confidentiality

▶   Will you be given any background information on the children you will work with? Are you aware of the importance of confidentiality in a childcare setting?

▶   This is particularly relevant if you are required to work with children with special or additional needs.

Attachment theory

▶   Why is this theory important in childcare and why it is relevant to your practice?

CHAPTER TWO

Developments in the ECCE Sector

In this chapter

- Development and growth of the ECCE sector
- Technology in the ECCE sector

The childcare sector in Ireland has grown dramatically in recent years. One of the challenges in developing a national policy for the provision of services for children aged from birth to 6 years has been the difficulty of separating childcare from early childhood education in relation to policy, funding, delivery and staffing.

Unlike the primary/secondary education system, which is clearly defined, services in Ireland that provide for the care and education of children aged from birth to 6 years include crèches, nurseries, parent and toddler groups, pre-schools, playgroups, after-school clubs and so on. This variety illustrates the range of purposes attributed to these services, including caring for the children of working parents and providing opportunities for early educational experiences for young children.

The current level of awareness and attention given to ECCE at national policy level is quite a recent development. Traditionally there was no universal provision of childcare or pre-school services. Outside the state-funded primary school system, investment in pre-school provision was traditionally targeted to support children in need of specific intervention, including those with material, social and educational disadvantage and children with special needs. The ECCE needs of babies, young children and their families were met in an unfocused way with a range of community and voluntary and private services. ECCE service provision was unregulated until 1997. When the Child Care Regulations came into effect, there was no requirement regarding the qualifications needed for childcare beyond a reference to 'appropriate experience in caring for children … and/or … an appropriate qualification' (DoHC 1996).

The non-planned development of services in the ECCE sector impacted directly on the practitioners who work in the ECCE sector. Many services, especially those provided by the community and voluntary sector relied heavily on volunteer staff. Even in the private for-profit sector, salaries were low and conditions of employment poor. Working in childcare was not generally viewed as a desirable career choice.

Up-to-date employment data sourced from the Central Statistics Office (CSO) and reported on by the Skills and Labour Market Research Unit of FÁS shows a major upward shift in the educational qualifications of people employed in childcare occupations. This is supported by a survey of the educational attainment of the workforce, commissioned in 2007/2008, which found that 41% of staff had attained a FETAC Level 5 qualification in childcare and only 12% of staff had no formal childcare qualifications.

The era from 1990 to the present day has been characterised by dramatic changes in all aspects of life in Ireland. According to the CSO, the population has grown from 3.6 million in 1996 to 4.2 million at present. The number of children aged under 6 rose from 256,703 in 1996 to 458,900 in 2012. The number of non-Irish nationals living in Ireland grew from 224,261 persons in 2002 to 544,357 in 2011, an increase of 143% over the nine-year period.

The two contributing factors were a continuous increase in the number of births and inward migration. Until mid-2008, the Irish economy grew at an unprecedented rate. Women's participation in the workforce, which has lagged behind our European counterparts, reached 55.1% in 2007 compared to 35.8% in 1990. By 2008 there were 921,600 women in employment in Ireland (compared to 1,186,900 men), an employment rate of 60.5%. However, during the economic crisis the figure dropped significantly and by 2011 had fallen to 56%.

The universal provision of a pre-school place for every child in their year prior to starting primary school was announced in the April 2009 budget.

The United Nations Convention on the Rights of the Child (UNCRC) (to which Ireland signed up in 1992) promotes the recognition of the rights of children, and there have been a number of declarations and conventions on the rights of children. The Irish government's vision, as set out in the 10-year National Children's Strategy is:

> An Ireland where children are respected as young citizens with a valued contribution to make and a voice of their own; where all children are cherished and supported by family and the wider society; where they enjoy a fulfilling childhood and realise their potential. (DoHC 2000:4)

Recent policy developments promote the importance of regarding the early childhood period from birth to 6 years as an important time in a child's life and as a time when the child has specific care and education needs.

INCLUSIVE SERVICES

The level of immigration in Ireland has highlighted the need for inclusive services that reflect equal opportunities for all children. The Salamanca World Statement, signed by 92 governments, states:

> Inclusion and participation are essential to human dignity and to the enjoyment and exercise of human rights. Within the field of education this is reflected in the development of strategies that seek to bring about a genuine equalisation of opportunity. (UNESCO 1994:11)

Do some research into the United Nations Educational, Scientific and Cultural Organisation (UNESCO) to understand its role. A good place to start is its website, www.unesco.org.

People who work with children and their families are faced with an increasingly multi-faceted population in Ireland, which includes variables such as social class, gender, returned Irish, family status, people with disabilities, gay and lesbian people in families/parents, ethnic minorities, the Traveller community, economic migrants, refugees, asylum seekers, Irish language speakers, non-native language speakers, religious minorities, the majority population and many others.

These differences are not in themselves problematic, but how people react to and construct meanings about differences could present problems or raise areas of concern. When we consider equality we must also consider diversity and discrimination. For those of us who work in childcare it is especially important that we have an understanding of immigrant parents and their children and that we ensure that they have equality of opportunity in our service provision.

To learn how to embrace diversity effectively in our practice, we must look at how we view difference in our own thinking and how this influences our childcare practice. What are our inbuilt values, judgements and values in relation to difference? We should examine our own practice to ensure that the children we work with have the opportunity to develop to their full potential in a fully inclusive environment.

Difference tends to have negative connotations, but diversity is potentially a great source of vital learning and interaction for our children. Childcare practitioners should regularly critically reflect on their practice and understand that their role in childcare is first of all to recognise that their job is to nurture and care for all the children they work with. It is important to understand that the children we work with must be valued and respected.

Childcare practitioners should be well informed about each individual child they work with, understanding their culture and background and meeting each child's strengths and needs. This is just as important for children from the majority culture as for those from minority groups. Diversity is a great thing; it enriches Irish society and culture. The greater our understanding and appreciation of difference, the more our society as a whole will benefit and grow.

Young children enter the childcare environment not as blank slates but with a general awareness of difference. Childcare practitioners need to acknowledge this awareness and the reality that diversity, equality and anti-discriminatory issues are part of everyday life in the childcare setting. Embracing and working with a diversity and equality approach is integral to the provision of high-quality childcare practice.

Points to consider in our practice to challenge discrimination and prejudice in a childcare service:

▸ What can I do to enable children and others to stand up to discrimination? How do I do this effectively? How can I role model appropriate ways to challenge prejudice and discrimination?

▸ Does my childcare setting reflect and include all children in its day-to-day activities? Are there representations of diversity? Are there books and toys that positively represent disability? Are the toys and activities gender neutral (e.g. not having a pink kitchen in the home corner)?

▸ Does my childcare service support the home culture of the child? Is this reflected in the pictures, art, toys, books, etc. in the service?

▸ Are non-verbal forms of communication used, along with verbal? Are pictures used to augment communication?

▸ We need to recognise negative attitudes when they arise and consider ways to change them. Thinking about working with children who present with challenging behaviours, what can you do to support the child with their behaviour?

▸ Reflect on everything the children experience in the service to identify any bias.

▸ Ensure that routine activities offer opportunities to reflect diversity of background, religion, skin colour, family structures, language, culture or disability in a positive way that will help all become aware of and respectful of differences.

Source: adapted from DCYA (2006).

EMERGING TECHNOLOGY IN THE ECCE SECTOR

The term 'emerging technology' refers to recent developments in information and communication technology and includes the use of social media and new hardware such as tablet computers and interactive whiteboards. There has long been a debate about the use of media, from television to YouTube, for education.

> Social media include Twitter, Facebook, YouTube, Pinterest, etc.

In his book *The Tipping Point* (2000), Malcolm Gladwell details how television came to become a tool for teaching literacy. In the late 1960s the children's programme *Sesame Street* was created to improve the literacy levels of children from disadvantaged backgrounds. The programme, which was aimed at both adults and children, used hand puppets and large walking puppets as well as adults and children to act out the scenes. The producers of the show wanted to discover if the programme held the attention of pre-school children while trying to teach them the alphabet and basic reading techniques.

> *Sesame Street* is a children's programme created in the USA and broadcast worldwide. If you've never seen *Sesame Street*, why not try to find an episode on YouTube?

The psychologist Ed Palmer (APA 1975) devised a method of testing whether children were paying attention when they were watching *Sesame Street*. He called this method 'the Distracter'. He would play an episode of *Sesame Street* on a television while simultaneously displaying a slide show on a monitor beside the television. The image on the monitor changed every 7.5 seconds. The researchers would sit quietly while the programme played and note any loss of attention from the programme. The first findings showed that some parts of the programme did not hold children's attention: for example, when adults were talking all at once to indicate excitement about a topic or storyline, it seemed that this confused the children and thus lost their attention. As a result, the programme format was changed with more segments that held pre-schoolers' attention, such as puppets talking on the television screen without adults in the shot. Although this method uncovered what the children were interested in, it didn't determine whether they were paying attention to the literacy elements of the show or, indeed, whether they were learning anything.

Further research was designed by another psychologist that used eye movement tracking to see what children watched on the screen, for example when a puppet spoke the letters H-U-G as they were centred on the screen or the letters C-A-T as they moved across the screen. Again, results were mixed and seemed to depend on whether the word was static (in the HUG example) or moving (in the CAT example). Can you guess which was more successful?

> The HUG example – static text with the puppet saying the H – U – G sounds – was more successful. Have you ever seen the film *E.T. the Extra-Terrestrial*? There is a scene in the film where a young Drew Barrymore is sounding out the letters on the screen. ET learned how to speak using this method!

Following this early research there has been an ongoing debate about using media and technology as tools for teaching children. Whichever side of the debate you favour, it cannot be denied that technology surrounds children in the form of toys, television, computers, digital cameras and video recorders, mobile phones, smartphones, iPods, iPads and more. Whatever your personal views on technology, it is important to have some knowledge of the electronic tools that can be used to teach and enhance your practice.

Basic skills that childcare practitioners should possess include using digital cameras and video recorders to capture children's behaviour and learning throughout the day. Using smartphones to send photos and videos to parents throughout the day or week is an excellent way to ensure that parents are involved in the day-to-day activities of their children: a parent can see their child's progress and be able to tell the child that they saw them colouring or running during the day.

There are thousands of apps that are designed for pre-school children to use for entertainment and, most important, for learning. Word and letter games, jigsaws, matching card games, dressing-up games, driving games and many more are available. These apps offer a rich learning experience that promotes independent learning. In addition, some research shows that children share the experience of playing with iPad apps and games, thus learning how to negotiate their turn and learn from other children. Research has also shown that using apps and games can encourage children to pretend play. For example, in one study pre-school children played a game in which animated balloons floated across a sky. The researcher noted that other children watching the child playing the game began to pretend to chase and catch balloons in the room.

USING AN IPAD AS A LEARNING TOOL

Lots of children's popular programmes have iPad apps that will support interactive learning. Before children use any apps, you must evaluate their suitability including their content, ease of use, whether they are age appropriate, whether they include advertising, etc. Many apps are designed using a *constructivist* approach that builds and builds on children's learning. Choose apps that children will master easily, which will give them a sense of achievement. It is advisable to allow children to use apps on their own at first and then become involved in order to scaffold their learning.

> Visit the Apple iPad website to learn how to teach with iPads: www.apple.com/education/ipad/teaching-with-ipad/

Interactive whiteboards (IWBs) are now widely used in primary schools and there is no reason why they cannot be used in the ECCE sector. Laptops and iPads can be connected to IWBs, enabling games and apps to be shared with a larger group of children. Childcare practitioners can take photos and make videos that can also be played on the big screen for children's enjoyment and learning. Short videos about diversity, culture, well-being and more can be played to a room of children and built into curriculum design.

AN INTERACTIVE WHITEBOARD. NOTICE THE HEIGHT AT WHICH THE BOARD IS POSITIONED ON THE WALL.

You can also find useful resources on YouTube.com, but it is essential to preview any videos you might want to show children to make sure that they are not inappropriate. At the end of a video a number of video stills are sometimes presented as thumbnails for you to click on to go to another video. Be careful not to show these videos, as some can be very inappropriate for pre-school children.

Using a communication tool such as Skype on an IWB can be an exciting part of the day, if parents can call in from work. Of course, this will depend on parents' access to Skype and whether it will fit into their working environment, but perhaps one day of the year could be set as a day to Skype parents from the classroom. This could take some organisation, but it would be great fun for children to see their parents on a large screen.

Skype is a free online video calling and messaging service: www.skype.com.

Visual records of a child's progress can be recorded and burned onto DVDs for parents to keep. Childcare practitioners can also create podcasts for digital storytelling and add sound effects to capture the children's imagination while using puppets to act out the story. Recording an audio clip of baby's first words or songs and poems learned by older children can all add to a multimedia-rich experience for children and parents.

Technology can also be used for curriculum planning and administrative duties, such as planning rosters, printing colouring pages, printing photos, typing letters to parents, creating newsletters and more. It is also important to know how to use mobile phones to send and receive text messages for effective communication strategies with supervisors, colleagues, managers, tutors, etc. Social media can also be used to communicate in the ECCE setting so it is important to be aware of what tools are available and how and when to use them to communicate.

> Read Chapter 8 on communication for more information.

Questions

1. Consider any immigrant parents and children you work with on your placement. How can you find out what their needs and expectations are? How are you actively supporting them? How are you ensuring equality in your everyday practice? What differences/challenges are you encountering in practice?

2. Explain the terms *diversity, equality, difference,* respect and *reflection.*

3. In your work placement, how do you celebrate difference? From your observations, do children naturally accept difference? How do age, background and culture affect how children play together?

4. Examine your own values and beliefs. Write down your top three values. How do your values influence your personal beliefs? How do your values and beliefs influence your interactions with children in your placement? Are there any potential negative influences? Some examples of values might be *respect, care, excellence, fun, equality, honesty* and *reliability.*

5. An immigrant parent approaches you to complain about a co-worker's attitude towards their child. The parent explains that their child can become quite upset at drop-off time in the morning. They have observed your co-worker ignoring their child at drop-off time and rolling their eyes because the child is upset. What can you do? How can you alleviate this parent's concerns? Why do you think the parent has approached you?

6. Investigate what technology is available in your work placement. Have you seen any co-worker use technology? If there is limited use of technology in your childcare workplace setting, find out why. If you have good IT skills, how could you positively influence your co-workers to use technology?

CHAPTER THREE

Legislation Affecting the ECCE Sector

> **In this chapter**
>
> - Basic rights and responsibilities of the employer
> - Basic rights and responsibilities of the employee
> - Legislation on health and safety, discrimination, childcare, data protection, child protection and employment
> - The Child Care Regulations 2006
> - Contracts of employment
> - The role of unions in the ECCE sector

Legislation informs all practice in an ECCE setting. It is very important that you have a clear understanding of the legislation that relates to policies, procedures and practice in an ECCE setting. This chapter looks at the basic rights and responsibilities of employees and employers in the childcare setting, the role of unions and the institutional context of the childcare sector. The Child Care Act 1991 and the Child Care (Pre-School Services) Regulations 2006 will also be explored.

HEALTH AND SAFETY

The Safety, Health and Welfare at Work Act 2005 is the legislation that informs practice in all work situations. The Act outlines the roles and responsibilities of both the employee and employer in a work environment, and this includes ECCE settings.

The Health and Safety Authority (HSA) website (www.hsa.ie) contains lots of relevant information for the education setting and business owners. Take a look to see what further information is available to help you make sure you adhere to health and safety procedures.

Encourage your work placement service to sign up for social media accounts and follow the HSA to ensure they are aware of current issues regarding health and safety in the workplace.

Safety, Health and Welfare at Work Act 2005

The Safety, Health and Welfare at Work Act 2005 lays down the main criteria for ensuring the safety, health and welfare of people at work in any workplace (including ECCE services). The 2005 Act replaces the Safety, Health and Welfare at Work Act 1989.

The 2005 Act outlines the following:

▶ requirements for the control of safety and health at work

▶ the management, organisation and systems of work necessary to achieve those goals

▶ responsibilities and roles of employers, the self-employed, employees and others

▶ enforcement procedures to ensure that the goals are met.

The Act is split into two main sections: employers' duties and employees' duties.

Employers' duties

Employers are responsible for ensuring and maintaining a safe and healthy workplace. An employer's duties include:

▶ Managing and conducting all work activities so as to ensure the safety, health and welfare of people at work (including the prevention of improper conduct or behaviour likely to put employees at risk). In an ECCE setting this would include manual handling training and setting policies such as dignity and respect in the workplace.

▶ Designing, providing and maintaining a safe place of work that has safe access and egress, and uses plant and equipment that is safe and without risk to health. The equipment you use should be fit for purpose and maintained appropriately. In an ECCE setting equipment used could include cots, toys, cleaning equipment, etc.

▶ Prevention of risks from the use of any article or substance, or from exposure to physical agents, noise, vibration and ionising or other radiations. Cleaning chemicals and bodily fluids are potentially damaging and need to be handled with the appropriate training and equipment by staff who are properly trained. Instructions on cleaning chemicals should be followed closely and the practitioner should wear appropriate protective clothing, such as mask, apron and gloves, when required. All chemicals should be kept in their original container and stored according to the manufacturer's instructions. All chemicals should be stored in a locked cabinet. When changing nappies or cleaning up vomit or blood you should follow the service's policies and procedures, e.g. wearing gloves, using specific cleaning products and double bagging before disposing of or placing the waste material with hazardous waste.

▶ Planning, organising, performing, maintaining and, where appropriate, revising systems of work that are safe and without risk to health. Examples might be policies on double gloving when changing a nappy or cleaning up bodily fluids.

▶ Providing and maintaining welfare facilities for employees at the workplace. An employee is entitled to have somewhere to wash, access to a toilet and somewhere to eat their lunch.

▶ Providing information, instruction, training and supervision regarding safety and health to employees, which must be in a form, manner, and language that they are likely to understand, with follow-up to ensure that the training is being implemented in practice. Examples in an ECCE setting are first aid, manual handling, and hazard analysis and critical control point (HACCP) training in food hygiene.

▶ Co-operating with other employers who share the workplace so as to ensure that safety and health measures apply to all employees (including fixed-term and temporary workers) and providing employees with all relevant safety and health information. Although the 2005 Act refers to employees' safety, it does of course cover the health and safety needs of children attending an ECCE service.

▶ Providing appropriate protective equipment and clothing to the employees, e.g. gloves and aprons needed to change nappies.

▶ Preventing risks to other people at the place of work by developing a safety statement (see below).

▶ Ensuring that reportable accidents and dangerous occurrences are reported to the HSA. An incident report should also be completed if such an accident occurs in an ECCE setting.

> • What health and safety policies are in place in your work placement?
> • How readily available are your work placement's policies?
> • How often do staff in your work placement receive training?

Safety statement

All employers must carry out a risk assessment of the work environment to identify hazards or potential hazards, to assess the level of risk posed by these hazards or potential hazards, and to put in place strategies to minimise or eliminate the risk. The

employer must then prepare a written safety statement, outlining the hazards, risks and strategies needed to minimise or eliminate the risk. A safety statement should be included in every ECCE setting. The document must:

▶   identify potential hazards

▶   identify whether these hazards are high, medium or low risk

▶   list control measures to be taken to avoid the risks

▶   name those responsible for implementing and maintaining the control measures

▶   contain plans for dealing with an emergency or any serious and imminent risk

▶   list the names of the safety representatives (if any).

The table is a sample of what might be included in an ECCE setting's safety statement:

SAFETY STATEMENT GRID

Hazard	Risk	Risk level	Control measures	Who is responsible for implementing/ maintaining control measures?
Hot drinks	Burns to children and staff	Medium	No hot drinks allowed in rooms with children	Supervisor All staff
Vomit	Infection	Medium	Gloves and apron must be used when cleaning vomit. All waste products to be double bagged and placed in hazard waste disposal	All staff
Torn carpet on the stairs	Tripping	High	Carpet to be removed and replaced	Management to pay for new carpet Maintenance personnel to remove torn carpet
Traffic at drop-off and collection points	Injury to children, staff and parents	High	Designated parking spaces for drop off and collection Parents must collect children from the door of the service	Management to provide designated car parking spaces Management to develop policy on dropping off and collecting children

The Safety, Health and Welfare at Work Act 2005 emphasises the need for employers to manage safety and health in order to prevent workplace injuries and ill health. Most accidents in the workplace are caused by human error.

BeSMART

The HSA has introduced an online risk assessment tool that generates a safety statement for businesses, available at www.besmart.ie. Find out if your service knows about this free tool.

You just need to sign up for a free account; when you have registered, the online assessment tool will guide you through step-by-step questions and answers that are designed to help you discover potential risks in your business.

The user is asked what type of business they would like to assess. If you enter the word 'crèche' the website displays a list of categories that are particularly relevant to crèche/childcare facilities. At the end of the process a risk assessment is created and you can print it out, or save it and return to it later.

Why not sign up and produce your own risk assessment?

What are hazards?

To ensure safety and health in a workplace, employers and employees should be able to identify potential hazards. A hazard is defined as anything with the potential to cause harm. A checklist of typical workplace hazards in an ECCE setting is outlined below:

1. **Slips, trips and falls.** Torn carpets, toys not cleared up, water spills, etc.
2. **People falling from a height.** Windows should have safety locks so that children cannot climb out; window blind cords should be out of children's reach.
3. **Objects falling from a height** such as children throwing items out of a window!
4. Hazards associated with the **manual handling of loads**, e.g. picking up and carrying children.
5. Hazards from **plant and machinery**, e.g. exposure to dangerous moving parts.
6. **Mechanical handling:** particularly relevant if you are working with a child with a physical disability.
7. **The movement of vehicles**, especially when dropping off and collecting children.
8. **Fire and explosion:** relevant to a kitchen area, gas and to hazardous cleaning chemicals.
9. The use of **hazardous substances**, including cleaning chemicals.
10. Exposure to harmful levels of **noise**.
11. Hazards associated with **electricity**. All plugs should have safety covers.

12. **Unsuitable lighting levels.**
13. **Inadequate thermal environment** (i.e. too hot or too cold). Radiators and hot taps should be controlled by thermostats so that children/staff do not burn themselves.
14. **Human factors**, e.g. inadequate training, violence to staff, stress, bullying at work. Staff should be trained in fire safety, and in the safe use of equipment, for example kitchen equipment (mixers, washing machines, dishwashers, etc.).

Identifying risk

When you have identified the hazards or potential hazards, you now have to assess the level of risk: how likely it is that harm will occur? What would be the consequences of the hazard happening? You can then categorise the risks, for example: lifting a child – high risk of injury; hot drinks being in a childcare room – medium risk of burns; flooding – low risk. This enables you to prioritise the measures necessary to ensure safety, health and welfare at your ECCE workplace.

Strategies

It is important to identify the strategies and/or resources needed to minimise or eliminate risk.

The ECCE service should endeavour, where possible, to prevent risks and should evaluate the risks that are unavoidable (such as a child getting sick). Policies and procedures on safe work practice assist in the development of systems of work that support best practice in relation to safety and health in the workplace. It is very important to provide appropriate training and instructions to employees in areas such as manual handling, first aid and HACCP for food preparation.

The safety statement should be reviewed regularly and, if necessary, updated or amended when a new risk is identified or a change in work practices introduced (e.g. new equipment or materials) or when an accident, or a 'near miss', has happened. The safety statement must also be revised within 30 days if directed by a safety inspector.

Employees' duties

All employees, whether they work full or part time, are permanent or temporary, have duties laid down by the Act.

Employees **must**:

▶ comply with relevant policies and procedures and legislation relevant to the ECCE setting and protect their own safety and health, as well as the safety and health of anyone who may be affected by their acts or omissions at work – which includes the children they work with

▶ co-operate with their employer with regard to safety, health and welfare at work

▶ participate in safety and health training offered by their employer

▶ make proper use of all machinery, tools, substances, etc. and of all personal protective equipment provided for use at work, including gloves, aprons and a uniform if necessary

▶ report any defects in the place of work, equipment, etc. which might endanger safety and health and make sure they are included in the safety statement.

Employees **must not**:

▶ be under the influence of any intoxicant while at work

▶ engage in any improper conduct that could endanger their own or anyone else's safety or health in the ECCE setting.

Consider how you comply with policies and procedures every day. Are you consciously aware of health and safety issues?

How would you handle a situation where you suspect a colleague to be under the influence of an intoxicating substance?

What is meant by improper conduct?

How are you asked to report hazards and safety issues? If a child falls, how is this recorded?

EQUALITY LEGISLATION

Issues relating to equality are very important in an ECCE setting. The Equality Authority is an independent state body that was established to make sure that everyone who lives in Ireland is treated equally, that there is equality of opportunity for all, and that people do not suffer unfair discrimination.

The Equality Authority provides information on equality legislation, and it can provide legal aid to people who wish to bring claims of unlawful discrimination.

The two pieces of legislation that deal with employment rights and that outlaw discrimination are the **Employment Equality Acts 1998 and 2011** and the **Equal Status Acts 2000 and 2011**. They outlaw discrimination in employment, vocational training, advertising, collective agreements and the provision of goods and services. Specifically, goods and services include: professional or trade services; health services; access to accommodation and education; facilities for banking; transport; and cultural activities.

The nine grounds of discrimination

Under the equality legislation discrimination based on any one of nine distinct grounds is unlawful. These grounds are:

▶ gender
▶ civil status
▶ family status
▶ sexual orientation
▶ religion
▶ age (does not apply to a person under 16)
▶ disability
▶ race
▶ membership of the Traveller community.

Discrimination is defined as less favourable treatment given to an individual or group of people. Discrimination is prejudice in action. A person is said to be discriminated against if he or she is treated less favourably than another is, has been or would be treated in a comparable situation on any of the nine grounds outlined above. To establish that discrimination has occurred, it must be possible to make a direct comparison. For example, in a case of discrimination on the grounds of disability, the comparison must be between a person/child who has a disability and another who has not, or between persons with different disabilities.

Indirect discrimination occurs if practices or policies do not appear to discriminate against one group more than another but actually have a discriminatory impact.

Each of the above areas needs to be considered in an ECCE practice.

▶ **Gender.** Most childcare workers are female. Does the childcare sector discriminate against male workers? How are gender roles represented in your childcare service? Do all the children have access to all the toys in your setting? What about the colours of different toys? Would a boy be uncomfortable about playing with a pink tea set because they have got the message that blue is for boys and pink is for girls? Gender-neutral colours should be used throughout the ECCE setting.

▶ **Civil status.** Some parents are married, others live together without being married, some live apart. It is important that all the children's parents' civil status is respected in an ECCE setting.

▶ **Family status.** What are the assumptions about family make-up in the ECCE setting? Is there an assumption that all 'normal' families are nuclear families (mother, father, married with children)? Families can take many different forms: lone parent family; re-constituted family; extended family; same-sex parents; and so on. Be careful about your assumptions of what a family is, be guided by the children and their families, and respect all family forms.

▶ **Sexual orientation.** Family members can be heterosexual, bisexual, homosexual or transgender.

▶ **Religion.** All religious practices and celebration days should be respected and reflected in the ECCE setting.

▶ **Age.** Children should be respected and consulted in the decision-making process in an ECCE setting. Staff should not assume that just because they are young their input and opinions do not matter.

▶ **Disability.** Concepts such as integration, inclusion and equality of opportunity are important here. The Education for Persons with Special Educational Needs Act 2004 and the Disability Act 2005 outline the right of a child with special needs to access education in an inclusive environment with children who present typically.

▶ **Race.** A child's ethnicity should be respected and reflected in the ECCE setting.

▶ **Membership of the Traveller community.** Children from the Traveller community and their families should be respected; the nomadic lifestyle of some Traveller families means that they require additional services and supports to facilitate participation in an ECCE setting.

The Equality Tribunal and the Equality Authority

The **Equality Authority** (www.equality.ie) is a statutory body set up to work towards the elimination of unlawful discrimination, to promote equality of opportunity and to provide information to the public on equality legislation. It can advise and support a person bringing a claim, but it has no power to decide a case.

THE EQUALITY AUTHORITY
AN tÚDARÁS COMHIONANNAIS

The role of the **Equality Tribunal** is to investigate or mediate claims of unlawful discrimination under the equality legislation. A mediator from the tribunal helps parties to reach a mediated agreement that is legally binding. If the parties object to mediation, a case can be heard by a tribunal equality officer, who can, after hearing evidence from both parties, issue a legally binding decision.

CONFIDENTIALITY AND THE DATA PROTECTION ACTS 1988 AND 2003

All staff in a childcare setting must respect a child's and their family's confidentiality. All documents/information relating to children and their parents/guardians should be stored in a safe place, preferably in a locked fireproof cabinet that can only be accessed by childcare staff.

It is important that you do not share information about any parent or child with any other people other than the staff and the service user. The only exception is if medical practitioners need to access the information in an emergency. If you are completing observations as part of your childcare study, you should not identify the children by name on your work; refer to the child as TC (target child). Even family members and friends must not be allowed to access information on the child without the prior permission of the service user.

Maintaining the confidentiality of the information in an ECCE setting is an important part of the role of a childcare practitioner. Confidentiality is also important to ensure the safety of the child and their family. Maintaining trust is a vital element in the reputation and professionalism of a childcare practitioner.

The ECCE setting is required to maintain data as part of the data protection legislation. The Office of the Data Protection Commissioner is responsible for upholding the privacy rights of individuals in relation to the processing of their personal data. An ECCE setting is required to keep information on the children currently and previously in their setting in a safe, locked and fireproof place until the child reaches the age of 21.

Visit the www.dataprotection.ie website to read more about data protection.
Consider what would happen if the confidentiality of data on children and their families in your service were to be breached.

These rights are set out in the Data Protection Acts 1988 and 2003. The Acts state that information about you or a child must be accurate and only made available to those that should have it and only used for specified purposes. A person has the right to access personal information relating to them and have any errors corrected or, in some cases, have the information erased.

EMPLOYMENT LAW

Union representation

Under the Irish Constitution any Irish citizen has the right to join a trade union. A trade union can provide an important source of information and protection on issues relating to employment and can negotiate with an employer for better pay, terms and conditions.

The Irish Congress of Trade Unions (ICTU) (www.ictu.ie) is the single umbrella organisation for trade unions. It represents the interests of a range of employees, both in Ireland and in Northern Ireland.

If a person is dismissed from their job due to trade union activity or membership it is viewed as being automatically unfair and an employee dismissed in such circumstances does not require any particular length of service in the job in order for their rights to be upheld.

The rate of subscription paid to a trade union is determined by the union, but is usually at the rate of 0.5% to 1% of the gross salary paid per year to an employee.

Pay

National Minimum Wage Act 2000

The National Minimum Wage Act 2000 set a national minimum wage. Since July 2011, the minimum hourly wage is €8.65 to adult employees over the age of 18 years with at least two years' previous employment experience. For teenagers under the age of 18, the minimum wage is €6.06 per hour. This increases after the first year of employment over the age of 18 to

€6.92, and after two years' employment experience over the age of 18 to €7.79. There are exceptions for employees who are close relations of the employer, and for those undertaking structured training schemes, such as apprenticeships.

To calculate an hourly rate, under Section 20 of the National Minimum Wage Act 2000 the basic method of calculation is to divide the gross pay a person receives by the total number of hours worked. To begin with, however, it is necessary to note what pay is taken into account, what hours are included as working hours and what is the pay reference period (over what period the calculation is made).

Visit the www.employmentrights.ie website to read more about:

- your rights and responsibilities as an employee
- part-time and fixed-term workers' rights
- working hours, leave, holidays and sick pay
- grievance and disciplinary issues, disputes and more.

According to the National Minimum Wages Act 2000, there are a number of items that are not to be included in the minimum wage calculation. These are:

- overtime premium
- call-out premium
- unsocial hours premium
- service pay
- tips which are placed in a central fund managed by the employer and paid as part of your wages
- premiums for working public holidays, Saturdays or Sundays
- allowances for special or additional duties
- on-call or standby allowances
- certain payments in relation to absences from work, for example sick pay, holiday pay or pay during health and safety leave
- payment connected with leaving the employment, including retirement
- contributions paid by the employer into any occupational pension scheme
- redundancy payments
- an advance payment of, for example, salary: the amount involved will be taken into account for the period in which it would normally have been paid
- payment in kind or benefit in kind, other than board and/or lodgings
- payment not connected with the person's employment
- compensation for injury or loss of tools
- award as part of a staff suggestion scheme
- loan by the employer to the employee

Source: www.irishstatutebook.ie/2000/en/act/pub/0005/ (accessed 29 October 2013).

Contracts of employment

A contract of employment is said to exist when there is a written or oral agreement between an employer and an employee with an overview of what the employee is required to do in the workplace and their terms and conditions. Anyone who works for an employer for a regular wage or salary automatically has a contract of employment. A complete contract does not have to be in writing, but an employee must be given a written statement of terms of employment within two months of the date they commence work.

Some employees have an open-ended contract of employment, which means that the contract continues until such time as the employer or employee ends it. Other employees work under fixed-term or specified-purpose contracts, which end on a specified date or when a specific task is completed.

Some terms are assumed by law to be part of the contract, for example the right to take maternity leave. These are part of the contract even if the employer and employee do not specifically include them. In other words, an employee's statutory rights do not have to be included in a contract to ensure his or her entitlement to them.

The Terms of Employment (Information) Act 1994 and 2001 provides that an employer is obliged to provide an employee with a written statement of terms of employment within the first two months of the commencement of employment. The statement of terms of employment must include the following information:

▶ full names of employer and employee

▶ employer's address

▶ place of work

▶ title of job or nature of work

▶ date the employment started

▶ if the contract is temporary, the expected duration of the contract

▶ if the contract of employment is for a fixed term, the details of the term

▶ details of rest periods and breaks as required by law

▶ rate of pay or method of calculating pay

▶ pay reference period (for the purposes of the National Minimum Wage Act 2000)

▶ pay intervals

▶ hours of work

▶ that the employee has the right to ask the employer for a written statement of his/her average hourly rate of pay as provided for in the National Minimum Wage Act 2000

◗ details of paid leave

◗ sick pay and pension (if any)

◗ period of notice to be given by employer or employee

◗ details of any collective agreements that may affect the employee's terms of employment.

Sample contract of employment

This is a contract of employment between [employer's name and address] and [employee's name and address] as from [commencement date]. This contract is an open-ended contract.

The position is Childcare Assistant at the [employer's name]. The duties of employment are outlined in the **Job Description**. Any other duties may be given to you from time to time as appropriate to your position.

You will **report to** the Childcare Leader and the Supervisor in your room, who reports to the Manager of the crèche.

You will be employed on a probationary basis for 6 months, reviewed after 3 months. Your probationary period will commence on your start date. Your supervisor will supervise your induction period of the first two weeks, when you will be supernumerary. After this ongoing meetings will take place between you and your supervisor to evaluate your performance and conduct and to provide support.

Your rate of pay will be € .... per hour. You will be paid weekly in arrears direct into your bank account. You will only be paid in respect of the hours you actually work.

Annual leave and public holidays shall be given in accordance with legislative requirements detailed in the Working Time Act 1977 and the Worker Protection Act 1991. In addition to public holidays you are entitled to 20 days' annual leave. Notice of annual leave requirements must be given 6 weeks in advance.

- Annual leave cannot be carried over to a new leave year without approval of the Manager.
- Where an employee has terminated their contract and the paid holidays already taken exceed the paid holiday entitlement on the date of termination, [employer's name] will deduct the excess holiday pay from the final termination payment.
- There is no provision to pay sick pay. You are required to ring in to the Manager by 8 a.m. on the first day of your illness if you are going to miss work. There is a maximum allowance of 3 consecutive uncertified sick days with a total of 7 uncertified sick days in any given year.

- Your employment may be terminated by 1 week's notice during the 6-month probationary period. After this period you are required to give 2 weeks' notice of resignation in writing.
- There are policies on grievance procedures, maternity leave, pension schemes, dignity & respect in the workplace, safety & health at work, code of behaviour, and other policies contained in the employee handbook. You are required to read each of the policies and to sign that you fully understand each of the policies and that you will implement them in your practice.
- Confidentiality in relation to your work needs to be maintained at all times. Breaches of confidentiality will result in the instigation of disciplinary procedures, which can result in dismissal.

Declaration of acceptance

'I accept an appointment as a childcare assistant with [employer's name], under the terms and conditions as set out above.'

Having read and fully understood them, I hereby accept the above terms and conditions of employment.

Signed: _____   Date_____
Employee

Signed:_____   Date_____
On behalf of Management

CHILD CARE ACT 1991

The primary legislation regulating child care policy that is relevant to an ECCE setting is the Child Care Act 1991. This legislation brought in regulations and accountability and considerable changes in relation to children and service provision in an ECCE setting.

Under the Child Care Act 1991, the Health Service Executive (HSE) has the statutory duty to inspect ECCE services to ensure that the regulations are adhered to. The HSE is also mandated to promote the welfare of children who are

not receiving adequate care and protection. (The definition of a child is a person under 18 years of age who is not or has not been married.)

The principles that guide the HSE in relation to the legislative requirements of the Child Care Act 1991 are as follows.

▶ It is typically in the best interests of the child to be brought up in his/her own family.

▶ The welfare principle dictates that the welfare of the child is the first and paramount consideration and, as far as is possible, the wishes of the child should be considered in decisions that directly affect them (advocacy can be used here).

▶ The HSE is required to identify children who are not getting appropriate care, attention and protection and to co-ordinate information on children from all stakeholders.

▶ The HSE will endeavour to provide childcare and family support services to support the family to support the child/children and to avoid the need for children to be taken into care.

▶ The HSE will prepare an annual report on the adequacy of the childcare and family support services.

THE CHILD CARE REGULATIONS

The Child Care (Pre-School Services) (No. 2) Regulations 2006 and the Child Care (Pre-School Services) (No 2) (Amendment) Regulations 2006 were developed following the Child Care Act 1991 part VII. They describe the measures that have to be in place in order to meet the requirements of the 1991 Child Care Act. An explanatory guide on the Regulations is available that gives guidance on best practice in relation to the measures outlined by the Regulations. Best practice includes the following.

Health, welfare and development of the child

Any person carrying out an ECCE service with a pre-school provision should ensure that each child's learning, development and well-being is provided for in the day-to-day activities of the ECCE service. The setting should provide appropriate opportunities, experiences, activities, interaction, materials and equipment for the children attending the service. They must also take into consideration the age and stage of the development of the child and the child's cultural context.

First aid and medical assistance

Each service should have an appropriately equipped first-aid box for children and with the information needed and protocols in place to get appropriate medical care in an emergency.

Management and staffing ratios

The Childcare Act 1991 includes specific requirements in relation to adult:child ratios according to the age of the child and the type of service they are in. The adults must be deemed suitable (over 18 and Garda vetted) and competent: at least half the adults in a setting must have qualifications in childcare and all adults should have adequate and appropriate experience in caring for children under 6 years.

There should be appropriate vetting of all staff, students and volunteers who have access to a child by obtaining references (at least two references are required by most services) and Garda vetting.

Adult/child and space ratios

Pre-school service	Age of children	No. of adults	No. of children	Floor area per child
Sessional services	0–1 year	1	3	2m²; max. 20 children per room
	1–2.5 years	1	5	2m²; max. 20 children per room
	2.5–6 years	1	11	2m²; max. 20 children per room
Full-/part-time day care*	0–1 year	1	3	3.5m²
	1–2 years	1	5	2.8m²
	2–3 years	1	6	2.35m²
	3–6 years	1	8	2.3m²
Drop-in centres	0–6 years	1	4 (max. 2 if under 15 months)	2m²; max. 24 children per room
Childminders	0–6 years	1	5 (including his/her own)	No more than 2 children under 15 months
Overnight pre-school service	0–1 years	1	3	
	1–6 years	1	5	

*When a full day care service also takes children not on a full day basis, sessional service adult numbers apply.

The HSE has the authority to limit the maximum number of pre-school children who can be catered for at the same time. This is to ensure that there is no over-crowding in pre-school services. If the HSE proposes to limit numbers, the provider will be notified and has the opportunity to appeal or make representations about this decision.

Behaviour management

An ECCE setting must make sure that under no circumstances is corporal punishment used on any child attending the service. There must be written policies and procedures to deal with and to manage a child's challenging behaviour and to assist the child to manage his or her behaviour. Techniques such as positive reinforcement, redirection and diversion are appropriate methods of managing behaviour in an ECCE setting (see Chapter 8).

Register of pre-school children ratios

Each ECCE service should keep a register with all the details of each child attending the service, including the child's name, date of birth, contact numbers for parents and any person who is nominated to collect the child, any medical conditions the child may have and the name and contact details of the child's doctor(s).

Information for parents

An ECCE setting should include parents in the care of their children in the setting. Parents should be given information about the service, including details of the person in charge and other staff, the adult:child ratios, the maximum numbers and age range of the children, the type of care, facilities, opening hours and fees. All this information can be included in a handbook, but increasingly it is made available on the ECCE service's website.

Premises and facilities

ECCE service providers, including pre-school services, childminders, drop-in centres, crèches, etc., are all required to make sure that their service provision meets certain criteria and standards that provide specific facilities:

▶ The physical environment and the premises must be of sound and stable structure and appropriate for the provision of the ECCE services.

▶ The Childcare Act 1991 outlines specific space requirements per child in an ECCE premises.

▶ All fixtures, fittings and the building and contents are to be kept in a good state of repair, clean and hygienic, in good condition and protected from infestation.

▶ The furniture, play and work surfaces should be clean, suitable and non-toxic and kept in an appropriate state of repair.

▶ An ECCE setting should ensure that there are adequate and suitable facilities for children to play, both indoors and outdoors, and to rest if needed during the day.

▶ Pre-school childcare providers must ensure that the building has suitable and adequate heating, ventilation and lighting; sanitary accommodation; and waste storage and disposal.

Safety measures

▶ There must be policies and procedures outlining what to do if there is a fire and how to extinguish a fire if necessary. There must be staff training on the use of fire equipment and on evacuation procedures. Both the staff and the children attending the service should know the fire evacuation and other procedures.

▶ All radiators in the ECCE premises should have fixed guards and be thermostatically controlled.

▶ All outdoor areas should be risk assessed and gardens and play areas should be fenced and doors and gates secured to prevent children straying or running out in public areas such as the road.

▶ All ponds, pits and other hazards need to be risk assessed and included in the safety statement and they should be fenced off to ensure children's safety.

> Find out how often fire drills are held in your work placement. Are you trained in using fire extinguishers?

Food and drink

An ECCE setting must provide suitable, healthy, nutritious and varied meals that are sufficient for the children's needs. A childcare provider must ensure that they are aware of any allergies that children may have to foodstuff or ingredients. Services should also be aware of cultural differences and opinions concerning food. Drinks should always be available to children. There should be appropriate and suitable places to store, prepare, cook and serve food. If food is being prepared on the ECCE premises the person preparing the food should have HACCP training (food hygiene training that needs to be updated every two years). There should also be suitable eating utensils. Hand-washing, washing-up and sterilising facilities should also be provided.

> HACCP stands for hazard analysis and critical control point. The Food Safety Authority of Ireland (www. fsai.ie) has an advice line that provides information on a range of food safety issues. Visit the website to explore issues that affect the ECCE sector.

The Department of Health's Food and Nutrition Guidelines for Pre-School Services advise that children in day care for more than five hours per session (full day care) should be offered at least two snacks and two meals, including one hot meal. A sessional service must provide one small snack and one meal.

> Can you think of common and uncommon food allergies that children/adults may have? What cultural/ belief systems do some people have about food?

Insurance

The ECCE provider is required to ensure that all the children attending their service and all staff and visitors are adequately insured against injury when in their service. While you are on work placement, it is usually your college/course provider that will insure you.

CHILDREN FIRST

Children First: National Guidelines for the Protection and Welfare of Children (DCYA 2011) deals with the recognition, reporting and management of child safety concerns. It focuses on the duty to protect children from abuse and neglect. It states what needs to be done to keep children safe and what to do if you are concerned about the safety and welfare of a child. The guidelines set out specific protocols for people working with children about what to do if you suspect that a child is being abused or neglected.

All organisations, including government departments, schools, health services, religious bodies, public sector agencies, clubs and the leisure sector, funded organisations, private and voluntary bodies that are in contact with or providing services to children, have a corporate duty and responsibility to safeguard children by:

▶ promoting children's general welfare, health, development and safety

▶ adopting and consistently applying a safe and clearly defined method of recruiting and selecting staff and volunteers, which includes obtaining Garda vetting and references

▶ developing tailored policies and procedures in accordance with Children First for staff and volunteers who have reasonable grounds for concern about the safety and welfare of children involved with the organisation

▶ designating a person to act as a liaison with outside agencies and a resource person to any staff member or volunteer who has child protection and welfare concerns. The designated liaison person is responsible for reporting allegations or concerns of child abuse to the HSE, Children and Family Services or to An Garda Síochána

▶ ensuring that the organisation has clear written procedures on the action to be taken if allegations of abuse against employees/volunteers are made

▶ raising awareness in the organisation about potential risks to children's safety and welfare

▶ developing effective procedures for responding to accidents and complaints.

Source: adapted from *Children First: Key Messages* (www.dcya.gov.ie/documents/child_welfare_ protection/Children_First_-_Key_messages.pdf), accessed 31 October 2013.

Questions

1. Outline the basic rights and responsibilities of ECCE employees and employers.
2. Conduct a risk assessment of the childcare provider where you are completing your work placement. Was there anything that surprised you? What can you do to address any issues identified? What risks are easy to resolve?
3. Explain the nine grounds of discrimination. Have you ever witnessed/ experienced discrimination in the childcare sector? What would you do if you witnessed/experienced discrimination in the workplace?
4. Why is data protection important?
5. Summarise the legislation that relates specifically to children and childcare provision.
6. What precautions and procedures are followed when preparing food in your work placement? Are you aware of any allergies that children in your work placement have?
7. What is the role of a designated child protection officer?

Skills and Qualities of ECCE Workers

Read the scenarios below and discuss them with your tutor and classmates.

Scenario 1: The worried parent

Anna is 3 years old and she is a shy child. She usually needs some coaxing in the morning to join in with play activities. She can be quiet when her mother drops her off in the morning. Her mother is worried about Anna settling into the service and usually rings twice every morning to see if Anna is okay. Your supervisor has asked you to speak to her about Anna and to reassure her that Anna eventually settles in each morning.

Discuss

What skills and qualities do you think you need to deal with both Anna and her mother's concerns? How would you feel about your supervisor asking you to deal with Anna's mother?

Scenario 2: Boisterous school-age children

Tom and Billy are twins who attend after-school care in your placement. They are 10 years old and have lots of energy when they come in from school. You have observed that some of the younger children are a little frightened by the twins' boisterous behaviour.

Discuss

What skills and qualities do you need to deal with this situation?

Scenario 3: Late pick-ups

Mrs Black is consistently late collecting her 1-year-old child from your placement. Your manager has asked you to remind her about collection times and the consequences of being late to pick up her child.

Discuss

What do you think are the consequences of Mrs Black's actions? What skills and qualities do you need to manage and improve this situation? How will you react if Mrs Black is defensive and responds, 'It's only a couple of minutes!'? If you were the person who was always late, how would you react to your supervisor reminding you of the importance of timekeeping?

Scenario 4: The critical colleague

Geraldine has just begun her work experience and is nervous about making a good impression. She is working hard to build good working relationships with her colleagues, but there is one colleague she perceives to be critical of her practice. This is affecting Geraldine's confidence. Geraldine feels that this colleague comments negatively on everything she does; for example, she has told Geraldine to smile more when speaking to the children in the service and that she should arrive earlier and leave later than other staff in the service. Geraldine has discussed these comments with her classmates and written about the criticism in her journal. Geraldine thinks her colleague is deliberately trying to make life hard for her and is 'out to get her'.

Discuss

How would you deal with this situation? Is Geraldine correct in thinking that the colleague is 'out to get her'?

Having considered these scenarios you will have identified some of the skills and qualities needed in the childcare workplace. It is advisable that you conduct your own personal skills audit to identify whether you have the right attributes to work in childcare. When completing a skills audit you could consider the following skills.

Personal skills:

▶ patience

▶ communication

▶ empathy

▶ observant

▶ trusting

▶ fun

▶ confident

▶ approachable

▶ reliable

▶ organised

▶ kind

▶ willing to learn

▶ able to work on own initiative

▶ able to work as part of a team

Professional/technical skills:

▶ good timekeeping

▶ IT skills

▶ communication skills

▶ behaviour management

▶ HACCP (food handling training)

▶ first aid

▶ childcare training

▶ manual handling

> Discuss in class the meaning and application of these skills in the workplace.

Also consider what talents, skills and interests you have that could be a useful resource in your practice, for example gardening, computers, reading, crafts, music; and how they could be used in an ECCE setting.

When considering the qualities and skills of a childcare practitioner in a childcare service it is very important to consider what skills and qualities the children, parents, colleagues and owners of the service would like you to have. You can access a detailed skills audit on the CD with this book. Take some time to completing your skills audit and ask others for help if you are finding it difficult.

What have you learned in your childcare modules so far that you can link to your work practice? When you have read this chapter, consider whether there are any skills identified here that you do not feel you have or are not competent in. If there are, you will need to determine how you can learn or improve these skills. Setting goals to do this will help you improve your practice in the childcare setting. Improving your skillset during work placement is highly recommended to evidence learning and to track your development as an effective childcare practitioner. Look at the next section to determine how to set practical goals.

GOAL SETTING

What you get by achieving your goals is not as important as what you become by achieving your goals. (HENRY DAVID THOREAU)

Goal setting is a very important element of your work experience in childcare. Goals can be personal, professional, educational or community-related. Examples might be:

◗ Personal goals: improving your confidence and self-belief

◗ professional goals: improving listening skills to help you better reflect on your practice

◗ educational goals: achieving a FETAC Level 6 ECCE certificate or a Level 8 degree

◗ community related goals: volunteering for a community childcare group or a parent and toddler group.

Goals can be long term (up to 10 years), intermediate (three to five years) and short term (up to one year). When you identify goals and write them down you are far more likely to achieve those goals.

Activity

Read through this list of goal statements. What do you notice about them?

1. My tutor said that I should be more reflective.
2. I would like to gain a childcare qualification.
3. I need to stop shouting when the children get noisy.
4. I won't be so lazy with my course work.
5. I don't want to be stressed any more.
6. I won't leave my work until the last minute.
7. I want to get a good job.
8. I won't be late.
9. I wish I were the boss.
10. I want to improve my self-confidence.

Tutors: see www.gillmacmillan.ie/workpractice&experienceinchildcare for the answers to this activity.

SMART goals

SMART is a proven method of setting goals. Goals they should be:

▶   Specific
▶   Measurable
▶   Attainable
▶   Relevant
▶   Time-bound

Set specific goals

> It is not enough to take steps which may some day lead to a goal; each step must be itself a goal and a step likewise. (JOHANN WOLFGANG VON GOETHE)

Your goals for your work placement should be clear and well defined. If your goals are vague or generalised they can be unhelpful because they won't provide sufficient direction for you in your work placement. Your goals will help you learn how to be an effective childcare practitioner. So for your work placement you need to consider the specific goals you wish to achieve. Do you want to learn a specific task or skill, for example? Reflect on your skills audit, identify the skills you feel you need to improve, and set these as your specific goal/s for your work experience.

> See the skills audit template on the CD.

Set measurable goals

> In all things that you do, consider the end. (SOLON)

In your goals, include precise times, dates, and what you specifically want to achieve so that you can measure when and if you have achieved your goals. Decide whether your goals are long term, intermediate or short term. If your goal is simply 'To be more organised', how will you know when you have been successful? How will you measure if you have achieved your goal? For example, you could decide that you will be more organised in your college work, that you will complete a learner record by Friday every week you are in placement, and that you will develop an activity to do with the children every day.

Unless you can measure your success you cannot see the progress you make as you learn to implement best practice in the childcare setting you are doing your placement in.

Examples of how to measure goals

- I will create and save a letter using a word processor.
- I will prepare planned activities a week in advance to ensure that they run smoothly.
- I will ask my supervisor to rate my performance during an activity using a pre-designed rating system that I will design in order to check my skills development.
- I will achieve a distinction/merit/pass grade in a module I found challenging.

Assess your stress levels after putting effort into planning your weekly study schedule. Are they different from your stress levels when you did not plan your schedule?

Set attainable goals

> Success is about enjoying what you have and where you are, while pursuing achievable goals. (BO BENNETT)

Make sure that your goals are achievable. If you set goals that you have no hope of achieving or are too difficult, you are setting yourself up for failure and this can impact on your self-confidence and on your practice.

Make sure that the goals you set are meaningful to you and your work in an ECCE setting. By setting realistic yet challenging goals, you should achieve the balance you need. Your goals need to be negotiated with the service you are working in. There is no point setting a goal to work with a specific child or in a particular area if this cannot be facilitated in your work placement. Discussing your goals with your work placement supervisor will also help you to identify some areas you need to improve. Showing that you trust and welcome your supervisor's input into your training will also help build a rapport with your colleague(s). By opening communication lines you are demonstrating the desire to fit in with the team, thus in turn enabling your colleagues and supervisor to give valuable advice. Remember, they may also have faced the same challenges as you during their training and may be able to provide tips to reduce stress and improve your learning.

Set relevant goals

> If you don't know where you are going, you'll end up someplace else. (LAWRENCE PETER 'YOGI' BERRA)

Your goals should be relevant to working in the ECCE sector. Making your goals relevant to the ECCE sector enables you to improve your practice and skills when working with children. Your goals must also be relevant to you personally. Do not try to achieve goals that others think you should. Although friends, classmates, family and colleagues will offer advice to you during your training, you should always and only pick those goals that are personally relevant to you. Some suggestions that others may offer you may be valid goals, and you may need to improve on them, but you should prioritise what you feel is most important and achievable within a realistic time limit. Evaluate your skills audit and see which areas you specifically need to work on in your work placement.

Set time-bound goals

A goal is a dream with a deadline. (NAPOLEON HILL)

Your goals must have a deadline. This means that you know when you have achieved what you set out to learn. When you are working to a deadline, it keeps you focused within a time frame on what it is you want to achieve. For example, you could set goals for the first couple of hours of your placement, such as getting to know the names of the staff and children you will be working with, the layout of the building and the morning routine. Then set goals for the next 50 hours of your placement, such as developing your observation skills, writing a learner journal a week and completing three activities with the children. You could then set your goals for the completion of your placement so that you develop skills such as working on your own initiative or being organised.

Write down your SMART goals

Good writing is like a windowpane. (GEORGE ORWELL)

The physical act of writing down a goal makes it real and tangible. You are far more likely to follow through and achieve your goals if you write them down. You should frame your goals in the positive, using phrases like 'I will' instead of 'I would like to' or 'I might', for example 'I will learn how to read a story and use different props and tone of voice, even when other adults are listening.' Put your goals where you will see them to remind yourself every day of what it is you intend to do. Put them on your walls, desk, computer monitor, bathroom mirror or refrigerator as a constant reminder. Use your mobile phone to set reminders for goal deadlines. Share your goals with your tutor, classmates, friends and family. If you talk about your goals with others they can remind you of conversations you have had, prompting you to put more energy into achieving your goals. At times of stress, worry, procrastination or fatigue you may find this annoying, but remember that the people reminding you of your goals are doing so because they believe that you can achieve them; in other words, they are showing their support for you. Remember to thank the people who support you at different times during your learning.

Develop an action plan

Write down the individual steps you need to complete and achieve each of your goals, and then cross off each step as you complete it. You will know that you are making progress towards your ultimate goal as you see each step being achieved.

Keep at it!

My time is now. (JOHN TURNER)

Remember, goal setting is an ongoing activity, not just a means to an end. When you work in an area such as childcare, you are constantly striving to improve your practice. Build in reminders to keep yourself on track, and make regular time slots available to review your goals and to discuss them with your course tutor and your work-based supervisor as you go along. You might need to adjust your planning to reach your goals as you will find some goals easier to achieve than others. Your action plan is an important way of keeping you on track.

Key points

Goal setting is much more than simply saying you want something to happen. You need to define clearly exactly what you want to achieve. Understand why you want it in the first place and then consider how to achieve the goals. When you follow the SMART goal-setting model you can set goals with confidence and enjoy the satisfaction that comes with knowing that you achieved what you set out to do.
So ... what will you decide to accomplish today?

ASSESSING YOUR SKILLS

For the Work Experience Module FETAC Level 5 and Work Practice 5N1433 you must have a completed supervisor's report sheet. This report forms an important part of the overall assessment of Level 5 Work Experience 5N1356 for FETAC certification. It should be completed by a supervisor/manager who has observed the learner in the workplace. The workplace supervisor/manager indicates the learner's performance by placing a tick for each criterion under one of the following headings: Excellent (only to be used in cases of outstanding performance), Very Good, Good, Satisfactory, Unsatisfactory or Unable to Assess.

These are the criteria typically used to assess a candidate:

▶ **Timekeeping:** Timekeeping and attendance are very important elements of work in childcare. There is an adult:child ratio that needs to be adhered to in the ECCE sector, so it is vital that you are present at your designated start times. Ideally this means arriving with enough time to attend to your own needs before you are on duty, e.g. discussions with your supervisor/manager, going to the toilet, etc. You can directly affect how a child experiences their day in an ECCE service, not to mention the smooth day-to-day running of the service, by inconsistency in your attendance and timekeeping. Parents may also notice problems, which would affect the credibility of the service and your own professionalism. You need to agree the start and finishing times directly with your work placement.

▶ **Work undertaken:** A brief description of the work the learner has done in the ECCE setting. This should include the age of the children you are working with and the type of setting, and what work you actually do with the children.

▶ **Working independently while under general direction:** You should be able to work on your own initiative, receiving guidance when necessary. You should demonstrate your ability to work independently and to initiate and implement activities with the children to include story-telling, art and craft activities, role play and extend play in areas such as the home corner.

▶ **Meeting deadlines:** If you have been asked to complete an activity within a certain time frame you should do so. Keeping to the routine and the planned timetables is also important. You should meet regularly with your workplace supervisor to set goals and to agree activities and then evaluate the implementation and effectiveness of these activities.

▶ **Personal presentation:** You should dress appropriately. Some services will require you to wear a uniform; you should in any case be clean, neat and dressed appropriately for professional work in the childcare setting. Jewellery should be kept to a minimum.

▶ **Adherence to health, safety and other relevant regulations:** You should be familiar with the health and safety policy of the service you are completing your work placement in. Regulations about intimate care, food preparation, and the elimination/minimising of risks outlined on the safety statement should all be adhered to.

▸ **Demonstrate effective personal communication skills:** Making eye contact with the children you are working with, lowering yourself so that you are at their level, active listening and being respectful are all important elements of effective communication with the children you work with. In relation to your colleagues, you should consult and follow direction, asking for assistance if needed.

▸ **Demonstrate effective interpersonal communication skills:** Interpersonal skills are life skills we use every day. Understanding what the children are interested in helps develop a good interpersonal relationship with them. Getting involved in their activities and taking on board their input and views are also important elements of developing effective interpersonal skills. Developing empathy is very important for children; try to demonstrate empathy in your practice by understanding why something is important to the child you are working with. Problem-solving, being involved in decision-making and being confident are all important elements of effective interpersonal skills. Interpersonal skills such as patience, organisation, listening, empathy, kindness, trust, being approachable, demonstrating respect, making eye contact and so on should all be demonstrated in your practice in your work placement.

▸ **Demonstrate effective technological communication skills:** You should have some computer skills for working in an ECCE setting. You may need to complete bookings or reports, and to access information from a computer. You will also have to use a computer to complete your Childcare modules. eReaders, computer tablets, interactive whiteboards and educational software are all used in ECCE settings.

▸ **Acceptance of direction/criticism:** Constructive criticism is how we learn, and reflection allows us to consider the critique and to adapt and adjust our practice to incorporate our new learning. This enables us to move towards best practice when working with children.

The supervisor's report is dated and signed by both the learner and the workplace supervisor and verified by the tutor or teacher of the childcare course.

Questions

1. Complete the following table summarising the main characteristics of each type of childcare service.

Childcare service	Characteristics

2. Investigate the childcare services in your local area. Use the table below to analyse them.

Name of service	Type of service (or role and function)	No. of employees/ children	Ethos and curriculum

3. Draw up a table with the headings Parents, Children, Colleagues and Owners and list the skills/qualities each would expect or want a childcare practitioner to have. For example:

Parents	Children	Colleagues	Owners
Kindness	To be fun	Work on own initiative	Efficiency

4. **Goal statement:** I will learn the organisation's policies and procedures concerned with behaviour management.

    List the steps required in order to achieve this goal. How long do you think it would take you to achieve this goal? Do you think it is an achievable goal? Could you rephrase the statement to incorporate more learning?

5. **Goal statement:** I will learn to work as part of a team.

    Using the SMART guidelines, outline how you would achieve this goal, what challenges you might experience, and how you will know when you have achieved your goal of working as a team member.

6. **Goal statement:** I will set up and implement an activity to improve literacy skills in the 3–4 years age group.

Describe in detail the skills you would need to achieve this goal. What will you do if the activity does not have the effect that you had hoped? How will you measure the effectiveness of the activity? How will you respond to criticism with regard to the implementation of the task?

7.   Write down a personal long-term goal. How do you propose to achieve this goal? Use the SMART guidelines to plan how to reach your goal.

8.   **Personal SWOT analysis.** SWOT stands for Strengths, Weaknesses, Opportunities and Threats. We can use these categories to list our attributes. Perform a personal SWOT analysis, using the grid below to help. Explain the difference between a strength and an opportunity and a weakness and a threat.

Strengths	Weaknesses
Opportunities	Threats

9.   Why is it important to set goals?

10.   What strategies could you use to ensure that you receive an 'excellent' supervisor's report?

Some sample answers are available on www.gillmacmillan.ie.

Reflection

WHAT IS PERSONAL REFLECTION?

Personal reflection is a very important part of the work experience in childcare. When we are completing our work experience learner records we need to be able to reflect on our experiences and what we are learning in the childcare environment. We learn what to do and perhaps what not to do! Your experience in the work placement, along with the theory you learn as part of your course, should inform your practice. When working with children it is very important that we learn how to be a reflective practitioner; we need to be able to reflect on our experiences and to understand how to apply our learning to our practice.

To become a reflective practitioner we need to understand what reflective practice actually is and how it applies to our work on a daily basis. Aistear, the early years curriculum framework, focuses on the image of the holistic child and it outlines the importance of the reflective practitioner in the ECCE setting:

> Thinking about what you do, and how you do it and why, and then judging how well it went, is part of any professional's work. The reflective adult uses information about children's learning and development to think about his/her practice and to identify how to improve it. (NCCA 2009a: 77)

REFLECTIVE PRACTICE

Reflective practice is about being aware of our practice, asking questions and implementing change.

Self-awareness is essential to the reflective process; and reflection should be an integral part of our practice in an ECCE setting. Reflection is about being aware of our practice and being open to changing our practice. The childcare worker needs to be aware of their own inbuilt judgements, beliefs and values and how they can inform their practice.

Values

Principles or standards of behaviour; one's judgment of what is important in life. (WWW.OXFORDDICTIONARIES.COM)

People internalise the rules and experiences they grew up with, which then inform their values. We need to consider what informs our values and how they influence our practice with the children and parents we work with. Family values and beliefs must be understood and taken into account in a childcare setting. We need to value ourselves, the children we work with, the parents, the ethos of the service we work in and our colleagues.

Childcare practitioners should model appropriate cultural and social values and give time for reflective practices that empower them to deliver best practice and allow children to be effective learners. This helps children to develop holistically, nurtures a secure sense of who they are and promotes high self-esteem, which supports the child's learning and engagement in the ECCE setting.

Judgement

The ability to make considered decisions or come to sensible conclusions. (WWW.OXFORDDICTIONARIES.COM)

The childcare worker has to be able to make judgements, sometimes in a critical manner. Judgements are important in relation to our practice: we need to judge when a child is happy, interacting, socialising and playing appropriately for their age and stage of development. We do need to reflect, however, on what informs our judgements. We also need to consider the negative judgements we can sometimes make and how they can inform our practice, for example when we make assumptions and judgements about parenting.

Beliefs

An acceptance that something exists or is true, especially one without proof. (WWW.OXFORDDICTIONARIES.COM)

What is a belief? Are beliefs only religious beliefs or can they be broader, such as the belief that children should do what adults tell them, or that children should be 'seen and not heard'? What beliefs do you have?

Activity

Reflect on your own values, judgements and beliefs. How do they inform your practice? What are your expectations of the children that you work with? Reflect on what you expect from the children in relation to their behaviour and their participation in the activities in the ECCE setting. If you have a child with a learning disability in your service, how do your inbuilt values, beliefs and judgements affect the learning opportunities you provide for that child?

In reflective practice we need to be self-aware and question our inbuilt beliefs, values and attitudes; especially those that may conflict with best practice in a childcare setting.

Having reflected on what we do, the next challenge is to be willing, if necessary, to change our practice. If the childcare practitioner is not willing to change practice, there will be no benefits from undertaking the process: development will not be achieved and professional practice will not develop into better practice.

REFLECTION

Reflection involves describing, analysing and evaluating our thoughts, assumptions, beliefs, theories and actions (Fade 2005). Reflection is a skill that needs to be developed and which is enhanced through the experiences we gain in a work placement.

We shall consider different models of reflection and then examine how you can reflect on your own practice/work and learning while at the same time enhancing your own reflective skills.

What is reflection?

The image of looking at oneself in the mirror, which the word 'reflection' suggests, implies that we are conscious of what we are doing. Reflection is a word that is widely used but not always understood.

> **Class activity**
>
> Preparation is important in any learning situation, so before you begin your work experience placement, consider the type of childcare environment you will be working in. Is it a sessional service, a school, a crèche, an early intervention service or another type of service? What do you know about the service you will be working in? What skills would you need to have in such a service?

Each environment in a childcare setting is unique as it presents with a set number of individual children all participating in their designated setting. A crèche can typically have a number of 'rooms' including a baby room, a wobbler room, a toddler room and a sessional playschool, and they sometimes offer an after-school service. You might be working in a playschool with a particular curriculum, for example Montessori, HighScope or Waldorf Steiner.

The skills needed to work in each setting can be different, for example working with babies can be very different from working in a playschool room.

When you start your work experience you will need to participate actively by observing the children, the childcare practitioners, what works well; and then reflect on all these. What skills do the childcare workers evidence in their practice? You should record what you see in your work setting in your learner record. Every time you complete a learner record it is a learning opportunity.

There are different theoretical models of reflection you can use in your work placement and in your learner record. We will first examine the work of Donald Schön.

Reflection-in-action and reflection-on-action

Donald Schön (1987) identifies two types of reflection: reflection-in-action and reflection-on-action.

Reflection-in-action (thinking on your feet)

When working with children you have to be able to 'think on your feet': you don't often have the luxury of time to consider how to deal with a situation. For example, if a child is climbing up a bookcase to get the 'interesting' book at the top you need to intervene immediately to prevent an accident. So you ask/help the child to come down and select the required book for them. This reflection-in-action allows you to use your initiative and to deal with situations based on how you have learned to deal with them in the past.

Reflection-on-action (retrospective thinking)

You use this reflective process to consider new situations or to reflect on what you did and think of new ways of dealing with a particular situation. In the bookcase example above you would reflect after the event and consider what you could do to prevent the child from climbing the bookcase in future, perhaps by putting the interesting book on a lower shelf where all the children could reach it.

When reflecting on action, it is important to record a description of the incident, and it is advisable that the childcare student keeps a reflective diary, as we cannot rely on our memory for an accurate and detailed record of what happened. The childcare student should record details of incidents that either troubled or pleased them, writing them down as soon after the event as possible. The learner record is an important and appropriate tool to use here.

The process of writing a learner record promotes the qualities required for reflection – open-mindedness and motivation; and also the skills of self-awareness; description and observation; critical analysis and problem-solving; and synthesis and evaluation (Richardson & Maltby 1995).

This is, however, something which requires practice and knowledge before the student can become proficient – and an understanding of the reasoning behind it can help develop those skills.

> **Activity**
>
> Think about how you deal with situations in your work experience. How could you introduce reflection as part of your practice in the workplace? Refer specifically to reflection-on-action and reflection-in-action.

Becoming a reflective practitioner

For the childcare worker, effective learning does not generally happen unless you reflect. To do this effectively, you must examine a particular moment in time, think about it, go back over it and only then will you get new insights into different aspects of that situation. When you do this, you will learn something new.

Reflection is a form of thinking which is associated with deep thought, aimed at achieving better understanding about a situation. It contains a number of elements:

▶ **Making sense of our experiences:** We should learn from experiences. In reflection we analyse the experience, then attempt to 'make sense' of that experience.

▶ **Standing back:** It can be hard to reflect when we are in the middle of that experience. 'Standing back' enables us to have a better perspective on our experience, issue or action.

▶ **Repetition:** When reflecting we sometimes need to go over the event a number of times to get a broader perspective and ensure that we have missed nothing.

▶ **Factual account:** A factual account is required when reflecting so that we are clear about what we are reflecting on.

▶ **Clarity:** Reflection can bring clarity, just like a reflection in a mirror.

Making judgements

Reflection involves being balanced in our judgement and considering all perspectives. We need to be able to come to a conclusion and either be happy with how a situation was dealt with or see how to change or develop an approach, strategy or activity.

This process should enable you to come up with new ways to approach a situation differently next time. Then try out your new approach/ideas to see if they are effective. You then complete the learning cycle and start over again with a view to refining your actions. This is an ongoing process because we can never achieve perfection. We should consider alternative ways of doing things based on our learning from previous experiences.

In our work placements we build up experience in a gradual way. The reflective childcare student will develop reflective abilities during their placement. Reflection develops initially in a safe environment where the student is learning and mistakes are tolerated, such as in work experience. Learning is a process and we rarely achieve competence the first time we try to do something new! You can then reflect and discuss the decisions that were made during supervision sessions with your work-based supervisor or class tutor. Reflection should become integral to these sessions.

David Kolb

According to Kolb (1983), reflecting is an essential element of learning. This is shown through the experiential learning cycle illustrated below.

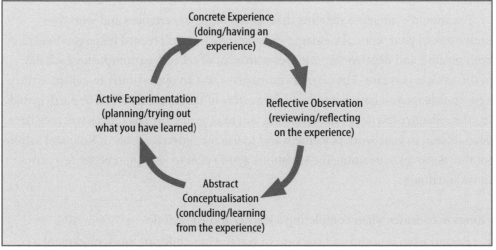

FIGURE 5.1 KOLB'S LEARNING CYCLE

▶ **Concrete experience:** Something that has happened to you or that you have done.

▶ **Reflective observation:** Reviewing the event or experience in your mind and exploring what you did and how you, and others, felt about it.

▶ **Abstract conceptualisation:** Developing an understanding of what happened by seeking more information and forming new ideas about ways of doing things in the future.

▶ **Active experimentation:** Examining new ways of dealing with the incident. Trying out the new ideas developed from learning from earlier experience and reflection.

The reflective childcare student must make time for reflection so that it becomes part of their – and ideally the childcare service provider's – way of working. Reflection should be an integral part of practice and childcare students need time to develop this skill. It is not a process that should be rushed. The student might reflect on their way to and from their placement, or between activities or during lunch break.

It is a good idea to summarise each day with a reflective comment in your learner record. If you do this every day you will be more likely to keep and benefit from your reflective learner record.

THE LEARNER RECORD

As part of your work experience you are required to keep a learner record which includes a reflective journal (see below) for the required 20 days (120 hours) of work experience.

You should complete a detailed description of the experiences and work you undertook in your work placement. The reflective learner's record helps you to explore both positive and negative experiences with a list of reflective prompts for each day of the work experience. The learner record gives you an opportunity to evidence the new knowledge you have gained and the variety of tasks you observed or participated in. The reflective learner's record enables you to examine the challenges you may have encountered in your work placement and to use the reflective tools of Kolb and Schön (outlined above) to examine the situations and to plan for new and better responses to those situations.

Things to consider when completing a learner record include:

▸ Record what is useful and relevant to you in your childcare work placement.

▸ The learner record should act as a cue to your memory.

▸ Make sure that you have a factual account of what you have seen and done.

▸ Ensure that you maintain confidentiality (i.e. use terms such as 'target child' (TC) rather than children's names).

A learner record can be used:

▸ to describe key activities and events in your work practice

▸ to evaluate key activities and events in your work practice

▸ to reflect on practice that may be habitual – things that are done because 'that is how we have always done it'

▸ to develop and explore what action was taken.

Getting started

▸ Set aside a time for writing every day.

▸ Try to complete a record for each day you do your work experience. Twenty records are required: one for each day of work experience.

▸ Allow time to think and to reflect on what you see or did.

▸ Do not worry about your style or presentation: you can always refine your learner record later.

▶ Remember that the aim of a learner record is to facilitate reflection on practice.

▶ Link what you see to the course material you are learning.

Reflective questions

Below are some questions you could consider when writing up your reflections on your practice in a learner record or when you are thinking back over an experience and discussing it with your work-based supervisor.

▶ What was I trying to achieve when I did ...?

▶ What exactly did I do? How would I describe it accurately?

▶ Why did I choose that particular reaction or action?

▶ What course material (e.g. theories/models/research) informed my actions?

▶ What were the consequences of my actions?

▶ What did I do next?

▶ What were the reasons for doing that?

▶ Did it work?

▶ What alternatives were there?

▶ Could I have dealt with the situation any better?

▶ How would I do it differently next time?

▶ What do I feel about the whole experience of being on work placement?

▶ What knowledge/values/skills did I demonstrate?

▶ How did the child/parent/childcare worker/supervisor feel about it?

▶ How do I know the child/parent/childcare worker/supervisor felt like that?

▶ What sense can I make of this in the light of my past experience?

▶ Has this changed the way I will do things in the future?

It is important to use the learner record to record positive experiences and achievements as well as the not so positive ones. A balanced view of what has taken place is essential.

Activity: reflection

Revisit the goals you set yourself in your skills audit at the beginning of the course: personal, interpersonal, technical and practical skills. Evaluate the skills and outline the skills you have developed. Are you reaching your goals in relation to the work experience? Have you any additional goals to add at this stage of your work experience? Remember that goals need to be achievable and realistic. They should be divided into short-, medium- and long-term goals so that progress can be tracked, adjustments made and goals achieved.

It is also important when reflecting to consider what goes well in your practice and to focus on the positives in what the childcare professionals do well. Reflection helps you to develop a problem-solving approach in your practice.

REFLECTIVE JOURNAL FOR WORK PLACEMENT

This student task plan is to help the student get a better understanding of what it is like to work in a childcare service/school. Students who are already working in a service could perhaps think about doing their work experience in a different type of service so that they can experience a broader range of the services currently on offer in Ireland.

Every childcare student completing the Early Childhood Care and Education Award FETAC Level 5/6 must complete a 20-day (120-hour) work placement in an ECCE setting. Some work placements facilitate hands-on experience; others require that you observe only. Either way, you can write in your reflective learner record about what you do or what you see being done in the ECCE setting. This record should be completed over the duration of your work experience. It is a required element of your assessment for the Work Experience module in Childcare.

Begin with an introduction outlining what you know about the ECCE setting in which you are completing your work experience. This introduction and reflective learner record should be completed during your actual work placement. The questions below will give you a template for examining the initial experience of being on work placement. You should then go on to complete the 20 daily accounts of your work placement using the questions to help you reflect on the many variables you will experience in the ECCE setting.

Section 1: Reflective questions during your work experience

Consider the following questions and complete them as you engage in your work placement.

▶ *The roles of staff in my placement setting are ...*

▶ *I was shown around the childcare setting/service/school and I saw ...*

▶ *In my first few days I was told about ...*

▶ *During my first week I was asked to ...*

▶ *Something I found difficult was ...*

▶ *One task I do in my day involves ...*

▶ *Something about work that surprised me is ...*

▶ *The equipment I have used so far includes ...*

▶ *If one of the staff is late for work ...*

▶ *One of the children in my group is ...*

▶ *All of the children in my group are ...*

▶ *Hygiene is important in this job because ...*

▶ *Staff ensure good standards of hygiene by ...*

▶ *Another member of staff was helpful to me when I ...*

▶ *What I enjoyed most was ...*

▶ *I would like to become better at ...*

▶ *I would like to find out more about ...*

Student daily record

DAY 1
Observe three children and identify what they like to do and which toys/equipment they choose during free play. Are there any boy/girl differences in preferences for activities? Gender roles and play are important considerations, and you should reflect on the toys provided in the ECCE setting. What do the toys reflect in relation to boys' and girls' play?

DAY 2
Ask about the fire drill. Write down what should happen when a fire drill takes place. What other health and safety considerations are there? For example, does your service have a safety statement?

DAY 3
Take note of the children's routine. Have they settled in well? Do they know what happens next at each stage of the day? Write down a typical daily routine, including times and your opinion of whether this routine is well established and how you feel it is working. Have you seen evidence of planning in the service? Is there a timetable of activities? What choices do the children have in relation to the activities they take part in? When children are upset, are they brought to activities which are known to soothe?

DAY 4
Compare two different age groups and observe what they enjoy doing. Write down at

least three examples of what each group likes to do and play. Compare the different forms of play: solitary play, parallel play and co-operative play.

DAY 5

Observe how children settle in when they arrive in the morning. Write down three different ways in which staff members greet children and involve them in activities. What examples of good practice are there in relation to how children are greeted and settle into their service?

DAY 6

Observe a disagreement between two children. Write down an account of how it started, what happened, and how it was resolved. What is the behaviour management policy of the ECCE setting you are in? Was positive reinforcement evident in the workplace setting?

DAY 7

Observe the tidy-up routine for the children in your placement service. Describe three ways of encouraging the children to help. Do they use songs to assist in this process? Do the adults help and encourage the children with this routine? Is there evidence that children are being taught how to participate in cleaning up?

DAY 8

Take note of the children's different language abilities: compare the understanding and type of language used by the children. What about the children whose first language is not English? What about the children who are only children or those who come from larger families? Describe the different approaches needed to deal with each of these children. Is there evidence of the use of posters in different languages? What books are available? Do the staff make an effort to learn how to greet children in different languages?

DAY 9

When the children go outside to play, take note of what the boys like to do and what the girls like to do. What do the adult carers do while the children are outdoors? Write down your observations. What are the health and safety considerations in outdoor play? How long do the children get to play outdoors? Are they allowed to move in and out whenever they wish?

DAY 10

Now that you are getting to know the children well, observe the different moods throughout the day. Are the children different in the morning and the afternoon? Does the day of the week make a difference? Have the children more energy in the morning than the evening? How does this inform planning activities in the ECCE setting?

DAY 11

You are now well settled in your placement. Select one aspect of the position you are shadowing which you have found interesting and discuss it in more detail. Have you a personal preference for a particular age group you have worked with? Is there a particular curriculum being used in your service? If so, how does it influence the service provision?

DAY 12

Is there a dress code for the position you are shadowing? Were you advised on what to wear before beginning your placement? Do the staff wear a uniform? What are the benefits of having a staff uniform?

DAY 13

Who discussed your daily duties with you? Were you given information about your expected start times, finish times, breaks and lunch times? Discuss how these things were worked out with the service. What support and direction have you received from the supervisor and childcare workers in your work placement?

DAY 14

Were you given an induction booklet for students/parents to read so that you could familiarise yourself with the service/school prior to or during your placement? Were you given access to any policies and procedures that would be relevant for your placement? Discuss in detail what happened in relation to this aspect of your placement. How important are policies and procedures in relation to practice?

DAY 15

Were you given any background information on any of the children you would be working with, either before or during your placement? This would be particularly relevant if you were required to work with children with special or additional needs. Discuss in detail how this information (if any) was given. Confidentiality can be an issue here, as a student may not be told a child's background; however, you can be given some information to help you care for a child. How does this information help you in your practice?

DAY 16

Now that you are coming towards the end of your placement, do you feel that this type of position is something you would like to work at in a full-time, permanent position? Discuss your favourite aspects of this type of work in detail. What did you find positive about your work experience? Was there a particular group of children you liked to work with more than another? Reflect on why this might be the case.

DAY 17

Were you allowed to work with any of the children in your care on your own? If you did not work on your own with a particular child or group of children, think about any activity you might have done with the children or a time when you worked on your own initiative.

DAY 18

Did you have a chance to observe some new procedures that you were perhaps unaware of before beginning your placement? You could refer to procedures such as changing a nappy, making up a bottle, preparing the children's snacks and so on.

DAY 19

Were you asked to be involved in any team meetings/staff discussions regarding any incidents/planning that took place while you were on placement? Some services hold staff meetings regularly: did you take part in any of these? Were there any discussions about the implementation of Aistear or adhering to the Síolta principles in your ECCE setting?

DAY 20

Were you asked to give specific help to any of the children while on placement? If yes, discuss what you were asked to do. You can reflect here on the difference you might have made to a child or children in your work placement. Did you support a child through a particular issue or activity? What did it feel like? Was your help/intervention successful?

Section 1: Reflective questions after your work experience

When you have completed your learner record you should complete the following reflective questions. These questions enable you to examine what you have learned about the role of the childcare worker and to examine the skills you developed over the 20 days.

- *New skills I have gained include ...*
- *Childcare workers/SNAs/classroom assistants are expected to ...*
- *On my last day ...*
- *Looking back on my placement experience, I think ...*
- *Something I liked about my placement experience was ...*
- *What I liked most about the other staff was ...*
- *The least enjoyable part of the work placement was ...*
- *Having completed my work experience, I have learned some things about myself: ...*

Complete this table by ticking the relevant boxes to evaluate your work.

	Excellent	Good	Fair	Comments
Attendance				
Time-keeping				
Getting on with my supervisor				
Getting on with other workers				
Ability to relate to the children				
Level of interest in the work				
Ability to use my own initiative				
Ability to do the work				

- *When I discussed my work experience and supervisor's report with my tutor/teacher:*
  - ◆ *I was pleased about ...*
  - ◆ *I was disappointed about ...*
- *If I were asked to give some advice to another student before going on placement, I would tell them ...*
- *In conclusion: Is this type of work for me?*

Compare your evaluation of your work experience with that of your supervisor's report sheet.

The Job Search

You are required to complete 120 hours' work experience in an ECCE setting as part of the FETAC Work Experience module in the FETAC Level 5 Early Childhood Care and Education certificate award. You should make sure that you have secured a placement, which you may have to source by yourself; or you may have the assistance of your course tutor.

GARDA CLEARANCE

As you are seeking a work placement with children you will need to have Garda clearance before you can commence your work experience. You should ensure that your college has applied for Garda clearance and you will need to complete a Garda vetting form. This form is typically given to you by the college and they apply on your behalf for Garda clearance. You need to do this well in advance of when  you expect to go on work placement as the turnaround time for this process can be months. When completing this form you must state all the addresses where you have lived, from your first to your present address, and you must not leave any gaps on the dates. It is a good idea to keep a copy of your Garda clearance form as you will need to complete this form for each childcare provider you work for. Once you are cleared you will receive a letter stating your clearance number. At the time of writing, clearance covers a two-year period and you will need to apply again at the end of that period.

INSURANCE

Your college should also provide you with a letter stating that you are covered by the college's public liability insurance. Most work placements require that you have insurance before they will accept you. The letter is typically from the insurer and clarifies who is insured and for how long the insurance is valid. A copy of the insurance confirmation letter should be given to your work placement.

SEARCHING FOR YOUR WORK PLACEMENT/ EMPLOYMENT

What you need:
- curriculum vitae (CV)
- cover letter
- interview skills
- a good online profile.

Before you start, consider your career goals and follow a plan that will help you to get the position that you want to have in five or ten years' time. Choosing the right job can be difficult when you are starting out and because you may have little experience you may choose the first job that comes your way. However, the main point to remember is that all experience should enhance your CV and it is up to you to recognise areas that you need to improve and to work on them in the workplace. This will give you evidence to improve your CV if you decide to move on to another position or apply for a promotion. Be strategic in your job searches and in your daily job. If you are aware of your weaknesses, work on them in the workplace. Eventually, they will not be weaknesses any more.

References

Referees are people who can vouch for your character, skills, abilities and experience. It is important to choose your referees wisely, and always ask permission before including their name and details on your CV. When applying for jobs it is courteous to inform the referees that they may get a call. This is, however, not always possible if you are sending off many CVs.

You may be asked for written references, so, if possible, obtain them before your job search begins. Remember that the referees you have chosen can be busy people and asking them for written references at short notice may not give them enough time to reflect on you and your skillset. Keep copies of any written references you have.

Choosing the right job for you

Think about what type of job or work placement is right for you. Do you want to work part time or full time? Are you in a position to work split shifts? Consider your own childcare needs (if relevant), the cost of travel to work, the distance and your transport needs. Do you want to work in a playschool, a crèche or a school? What is most important to you when looking for a job: location, working hours, work/life balance, challenges, working for a small or large organisation? It is advisable to be aware of your own needs when looking for job opportunities; if your own needs are met you are more likely to be an effective childcare practitioner whom an employer will be happy to employ.

> Take a moment now to consider what is the right job for you. What factors will influence your job search? Are there any sacrifices you are prepared to make to get a work placement or job? How will you arrange your life to fit around your course, work placement and/or job? What are you not willing to sacrifice and how will this affect you and your family?

CVs

It is very important to be able to write a good CV that tells the prospective employer all the information they need to know about you. This is the opportunity to 'sell' yourself to the potential employer, outlining clearly the skills and qualifications you have that would be an asset to their service.

A CV outlines your personal details, educational attainments, work experience, interests/hobbies and referees. It is a tool used to present your skills, achievements and experience. It needs to generate interest, engage the reader and make a clear connection between what you have to offer and what the employer needs. The CV also forms the foundation for a job interview.

When you write a CV the general rule of thumb is to start with the present and work back to what you have done in the past (reverse chronological order).

It might seem obvious, but a CV should be typed and be formatted using a word processor. There are many free word processing applications that are available (e.g. Google Drive), so don't worry if you don't own word processing software. You should use a sensible format and clear headings and make sure that your grammar and spelling are correct throughout your CV.

Writing the CV

CVs can follow a number of different formats, but the one we will be outlining here is the most common.

If you are posting your CV in response to a job advertisement, print it onto good-quality A4 paper, preferably not ordinary photocopying paper. You will most likely also have the option to email your CV.

Here are a few guidelines.

▶ Your CV should be no more than two pages long.

▶ Use a clear, standard font (e.g. Calibri, Verdana or Times Roman).

▶ Use font size 10 for paragraphs and bullet points and font size 12 for headings.

▶ Clearly differentiate headings and subheadings from blocks of text.

▶ Format your CV using bold and italic options.

▶ Use colour sparingly to indicate headings. Text colour must be black.

▶ Present your education and work experience in reverse chronological order, i.e. most recent first, making sure to highlight the areas of your education and previous work experience that are relevant to childcare.

▶ Check *very carefully* that there are no spelling/grammatical mistakes or typing errors. Use the spell checker, but don't rely on it!

▶ Show your CV to your tutor, a friend or colleague to check it and to get feedback.

Identify your skills

The key skills that are needed in childcare were examined in Chapter 4. You should already have completed a skills audit; if you haven't, look back to Chapter 4 and go through the audit. A job advertisement usually includes a description of the skills and qualifications needed for the job.

It is *essential* to be aware of these key skills before writing your CV. You need to identify the skills you have that could be relevant to an ECCE setting and to working with children.

Also consider what hobbies and interest you have that might be an asset in an ECCE service, for example being able to play a musical instrument, being able to sing, sew, knit, being good at arts and crafts, drama, dance, sport or any relevant volunteering you may have done. A simple way to display your skills is to list your education, work experience (full- and part-time), work placement and other activities, such as your interests and significant events in your life.

Sample CV

Mary Smith

Main Street, Drogheda, Co. Louth

marysmith@gmail.com

041 12345

086 123 4555

Personal Profile

I am a diligent and reliable person. I enjoy working as part of a team but can also work independently. I am an enthusiastic, fun and friendly childcare practitioner with a passion for early childhood care and education.

Educational Attainments

September 2013 to present

Dublin and Dún Laoghaire Education and Training Board, Sarsfield House, Balbriggan, Co. Dublin

Early Childhood Care and Education FETAC Level 5 Award modules completed:
Child Development, Early Care & Education Practice, Early Childhood Education & Play, Child Health & Wellbeing, Work Experience, Communications, Special Needs Assisting & School Age Childcare.

September 2007 to 2012

Local Community School, Main Street, Drogheda, Co. Louth

Leaving Certificate

English (Hons – C2), Geography (C3), French (C3), Irish (B1), Maths (C2), Business (Hons – D1), Biology (D1)

Work Experience

September 2013–present

Part-time relief work at Funny Bunnies Crèche, Dublin Street, Drogheda, Co. Louth

Duties

Working as required in both the baby room and the wobbler room, participating in the children's day-to-day routines and activities. This includes meeting their care needs such as nappy changing, feeding, cleaning and assisting with sleep routines. Their developmental/play needs are also provided for; I take part in their daily programmes, extending and facilitating play when necessary.

September 2013–present

Work Placement

I completed my work placement in Funny Bunnies crèche (120 hours) and they asked me to go on to their relief panel as outlined above.

Skills/Hobbies

- I have completed my ECDL computer licence and have a full clean driving licence.
- I volunteer with the local football club and help to train the 5- and 6-year olds in the local GAA club twice a week.
- I like to sing and belong to the local choir. I am also a member of the local drama society.

Referees

Ms Green	Ms Black
Principal, Local Community School	Funny Bunnies Crèche Manager
Main Street	Dublin Street
Drogheda	Drogheda
Co. Louth	Co. Louth
041 54321	087 334 4678

COVER LETTERS

You will need to include a cover letter with your CV when you apply for a job. This letter is very important as it is generally the first document your prospective employer reads. It is vital to make a clear connection between what you have to offer and the job requirements.

You should include your name and address and the name and address of the person you are writing to. If the job description does not include the name of the person you need to write to, ring the organisation to find out their name. It is much better to address the letter to a specific person than to 'Dear Sir or Madam'.

Sample cover letter

[your name and address]
Mary Smith
Main Street
Co. Louth

[name and address of the person you're writing to]
Ms Bernie Murray
Managing Director
Another Crèche,
Co. Louth

[date]
1 July 2014

[salutation]
Dear Ms Murray

[subject]
Re: Childcare Worker position

I wish to apply for the Childcare Worker position advertised in the *Irish Independent* on 29 June. I have worked in a childcare centre as a relief worker for the last 6 months and I have found it a very rewarding experience.

I am given the opportunity in this role to assist the children with their care needs and to take part in the play curriculum.

I am currently undertaking my Early Childhood Care and Education FETAC Level 5 Award, and I have completed the Child Development, Early Care and Education Practice, Early Childhood Education and Play, Child Health & Wellbeing, Special Needs Assisting and Work Experience modules. I have yet to complete the Communications and School Age Childcare modules, which I hope to complete in the next four weeks.

My sociable and friendly nature means that I have the ability to connect with children and adults from diverse backgrounds.

I have completed a First Aid certificate and have current Garda vetting approval. Attached please find my CV. Please let me know if you require further information.

I look forward to hearing from you.

Yours sincerely,

[your signature]
Mary Smith

APPLICATION FORMS

More and more employers use application forms in the recruitment process. The application form can be a fairer and more transparent way of recruiting staff because everyone fills out the same form and answers the same questions.

The form will ask for information about your skills, qualities, achievements and experience in the ECCE sector in a format the employer can compare with other applicants. If the potential employer has asked for an application form they usually do not require you to send a CV. Remember that the information you include on the application form will decide whether or not you are called for interview.

The best advice for filling out an application form is to prepare thoroughly. Read the form through from beginning to end before you write anything in. This will help you plan what information should be included where. Make sure to follow the instructions (e.g. using a black pen, writing in block capitals).

You will need to demonstrate that you have the qualities, skills, aptitude and temperament required to do the job. The best way to do this is to give an example of something you have done that illustrates these qualities or that helped you to develop them. Some application forms provide scenario-type questions, which give you the opportunity to show your knowledge and experience. (We shall look at scenario-type questions in the Job Interview section below.)

> Make one or more photocopies of the application form to practise filling it in.
> Also photocopy the finished application form so you can review it if you are called for an interview.

If the potential employer is seeking specific qualifications, such as a childcare award at FETAC Level 5 or 6 or a degree in ECCE at Level 7 or 8, be sure to make it clear that you have the required qualifications; also give a breakdown of the modules completed in your course.

Even if you have not worked in childcare previously you can relate your skills from another setting to the childcare job. For example, working in a shop may have helped you to develop good interpersonal, problem-solving and organisational skills, all of which are important skills in childcare. Use your contacts. Do you know anyone who already works at the service? If so, you could talk to them and find out about the setting.

Think through all the jobs you have done: training, childcare work, voluntary work. Consider the positions of responsibility that you have held. Also think about your studies and your hobbies and interests. Decide in each case whether there are any skills or aptitudes you can demonstrate that would be relevant to the job you are applying for.

Remember that the employer is probably comparing your application form with many others, so make the most of your experiences and achievements. For example, include any voluntary work, childminding or babysitting, and any hobbies that would be useful in a childcare setting, such as music, drama, art, sports or gardening.

Mention anything else you think might be important, such as any courses you have completed, for example first aid, manual handling or ECDL (European Computer Driving Licence), or if you have a full driving licence. Decide what is relevant and include it.

If you are offered an interview, the application form will probably be used by the interviewer as a basis for discussion, so keep a copy of the finished form, the advertisement, and your draft versions. You will need to re-read your application before an interview to remind yourself of what you said and how you said it.

Pay attention to detail, including spelling, grammar and punctuation. This is why completing a draft of your application is so important – it allows you to correct spelling and grammar if necessary.

You will generally be asked to include referees' names and contact details on the application form. Before giving someone's name as a referee get their permission and ask how they wish to be contacted, for example by email, phone or letter.

INTERPRETING THE JOB ADVERTISEMENT

It is vital to read the job advertisement carefully. What experience, personal qualities and qualifications is it asking for? This will usually be described in a 'person specification'. The person specification can sometimes be split into two categories – essential qualities/experience and desirable qualities/experience. You may not meet all the desired qualities; however, you should meet the essential qualities and experience.

The 'job description' section describes the role and its duties and responsibilities. Read through this carefully so that you know what the job entails. If there is neither a job description nor a person specification, you can still make an intelligent guess as to what the employer will be looking for by looking at the job description in detail and/or by doing some research about the ECCE setting online – it will almost certainly have a website.

Look for key words/phrases such as 'team player', 'works on own initiative', 'friendly' and so on.

> **Key words:** Team player, Diligent, Enthusiastic, Fun, Friendly, Reliable, Honest, Caring, Respectful, Creative

Redraft your CV to include these words or words with similar meanings. It is important to read your CV for each job application and match it to the job description and person specification. You may need to add more information to the CV to prove that you have the skills required for the job. The more you practise rearranging your CV the easier it will become and soon you will improve your CV-writing skills.

If you do not have the required educational attainments stated in the advertisement it is probably best not to apply, as you will not be considered. As a general rule of thumb, if you do not have 60% to 70% of the requirements, you will be excluded from the interview process. If training such as first aid, HACCP or manual handling is required, ensure that you have this too.

Reading job advertisements is also a good way to identify the kinds of skills and qualities that employers are looking for. If you are missing a qualification it may be a good idea to try to achieve this qualification.

Sample job advertisement 1

Pre-School Leader (Part-Time)
€ excellent DOE*

Our client is a leading childcare provider. An excellent opportunity has now arisen for a Pre-School Leader to join their team on a part-time basis.

This is the ideal role for a qualified pre-school professional looking to progress their career with a leading company. Joining a vibrant and friendly environment, the successful candidate will play a key role in the early years of the child, the smooth running of one of our client's crèches and continuous development of a group of children.

As a Pre-School Leader, you will be responsible for ensuring the development of children within the facility.

Focusing on the learning and development of children, you'll plan, design and implement a weekly scheme of work, to be delivered in the most effective manner, in consultation with the manager. Ensuring that all paperwork is handled promptly and efficiently, you'll complete daily record books, roll books, sign in and out sheets, cleaning sheets, outdoor play sheets and accident reports.

Additionally, you'll observe and report on the development of the children on a regular basis and ensure that parents are kept updated on their progress.

To be considered for this role, you must have:

- At least three years' work experience in the pre-school sector
- A BA in early education
- A nationally accredited award in early childhood care

As a Pre-School Leader, you must possess excellent communication, interpersonal and organisational skills. Adaptable and innovative, you must also have the desire to ensure the continuous learning and development of children.

*DOE means 'depending on experience'.

Sample job advertisement 2

Funny Bunnies Crèche is a leading provider of Childcare Centres in Ireland. Our respect for young children and their teachers creates an atmosphere of caring, delight and wonder that makes every Funny Bunnies Crèche a stimulating place where children, as well as carers, flourish.

Due to ongoing development, we currently have an opportunity for:

Bank Staff / Relief Cover /Full-Time Temp Childcare Worker

Required skills:

- Qualification in childcare: FETAC Level 5 and previous experience working in a childcare setting
- Team player
- Maintain professionalism in organisation
- Excellent interaction skills between staff and children

As a Childcare Practitioner you will be a key member of the Funny Bunnies Childcare team, being responsible for delivering high-quality care and learning opportunities for children, based on the needs and interests of those children. Some of your duties will be:

- Promote positive relationships with parents, children and colleagues
- Ensure health, safety and well-being of the children
- Support the children's development, learning and play
- Be a key person carrying out all related responsibilities in building relationships with a small group of children and their families according to Aistear

We offer our employees a good salary and benefits package which includes:

- Ongoing training
- Career development opportunities
- Loyalty programme
- Succession planning

Applicants must supply acceptable character references and be in a position to obtain Garda clearance.

For further information please apply with CV and a covering letter.

> **Activity**
>
> Examine the sample job advertisements and identify the key skills and qualities they ask for. How could you show that you have these skills and qualities in a CV, application form or at an interview? Compare the job descriptions and person specifications in each advertisement. Draft a CV and cover letter for each advertisement.

THE JOB INTERVIEW

If you are called for interview it is very important to research the childcare facility where you are being interviewed. You should know the following:

▶ How many children there are in the service.

▶ What type of services they provide.

▶ Approximately how many staff there are.

▶ The curriculum they use.

▶ The qualifications required for the job.

You should also make sure that you know where the interview is and do a trial run of the journey before the interview to make sure you know how long it will take to get there.

Prepare yourself a day or two before your interview. Read over the advertisement again before you go for your interview. Print and read your CV/application form and cover letter. Practise your greeting, answering potential interview questions, and sitting still and comfortably in a chair.

On the day of the interview, try to arrive about 10–15 minutes early. This will give you time to refresh your appearance and calm your nerves. Remember to be courteous to everyone you meet at the premises – the interviewer may overhear receptionists greeting you.

First impressions are very important, so make an effort with your presentation. Your clothes should be smart and formal for an interview. It is best to wear a suit for an interview; if you are a woman, make sure that your skirt is knee length or below – no mini-skirts! If you don't own a suit, perhaps you could borrow one from a friend. You should make sure that you are clean/clean-shaven, well rested and fresh for your interview. If you tend to perspire when you are nervous, wear lighter clothes and use a good deodorant. Don't wear too much make-up or perfume/cologne. If you have any facial piercings, consider taking them out as they could be a potential safety risk (if they fall out a child could put them in their mouth).

Your body language is also very important. Make eye contact with the people interviewing you and offer each of them a firm handshake. If you are inclined to fidget it can be a good idea to bring a folder with references into the interview with you – this gives you something to hold while you are being interviewed.

The interviewer/s will typically use either your CV or your application form as a basis for the interview and they then ask you a series of questions (some examples of which are outlined in the next section).

Interview questions

Why not practise answering these questions in class or with a friend? If you have a smartphone or iPad, record yourself and your answers so that you can hear what you sound like when answering these questions. This will enable you to analyse your tone of voice. For example, if you are claiming to be a fun person, it might be expected that you would be an animated speaker, but if you can hear that your voice is a monotone this will not convey a fun person! Give it a try – no one else has to listen to it, just you.

Opening questions: personal information

Could you tell me a little bit about yourself? See every question as an opportunity to sell yourself, so if you are asked this question make a link between you and the job you are interviewing for. You might want to tell them about your course, your experience of working with children or your voluntary work.

What interests you about working in childcare? This gives you an opportunity to explain what it is that you find interesting and rewarding around working with children. You could talk about supporting children's development, making a difference in a child's life, enjoying the planning and engagement in childcare activities and so on.

What is it that sets you apart from other applicants applying for this position? You need to discuss your specific skills here. You might have an additional language. You could refer back to the skills audit you did earlier in this book and talk about, for example, being organised, kind, empathetic, patient, being able to play a musical instrument and so on. You should give some examples of how you demonstrate your skills. Do not sell yourself short!

What are your greatest strengths, both as an employee and as an individual? This links to the last question but is framed differently. Be clear before you go to an interview what you are good at, and provide examples. You could talk about good interpersonal skills, being comfortable communicating and engaging with children, parents and colleagues alike –provided, of course, that this actually is one of your strengths.

What are your weak points? We all have areas that we need to improve upon, but it is probably best not to dwell on these in an interview. You could reflect on an area you are aware of that you need to work on, but stress how you have developed strategies to improve this area. An example of this might be that you are aware of the importance of organisation in a childcare setting, that this is something that did not come naturally to you, that you have had to work on it and that you are much better organised now.

What did you think of your previous employer?/Tell me about your previous employer. You should never criticise a former employer. Reflect on a positive aspect of your previous employment; for example, you could say that they supported your training or that you learned so much about children in your previous work placement.

Why did you leave your previous job? Be honest without being critical. You could say, for example, that you wanted to create better opportunities for yourself professionally.

What are your hobbies and interests? Like the first question, this gives you an opportunity to tell the employer why they should hire you. You should, if you can, make a link to your hobbies and interests and how they could potentially be a resource for the ECCE service. Gardening is a good example of this as many services are developing outdoor gardens and many primary schools are participating in the Green Flag programmes.

Educational requirements

What relevant educational qualifications do you have for work in this sector? Refer here to your course modules and explain how they link to the job requirements. If you have additional qualifications that could be important, particularly in IT, business, first aid, HACCP, child protection or manual handling, make sure that you mention them. What have you learned in your childcare course that you could apply to your work in childcare? Make links with your knowledge of child development, curricula, the theory of play, Aistear, Síolta, behaviour management, legislation, etc.

Experience

What experience do you have of working in the childcare sector? Mention your work placement, any voluntary work you have done or do with children, if you have been a child minder or, indeed, if you have children of your own.

What aspects of your work placement did you most enjoy? This should be easy to answer – if you are looking for a job in childcare you must have had positive experiences in your work placement. You learner records should help you here, with reflections on the activities you engaged in with the children you worked with and also on the learning experiences you engaged in.

Which of your past employers most impressed you as a manager? How did they earn your respect? You could refer to different management styles here. You might, for instance, reflect on a democratic management style that facilitated the involvement of all staff in decision making at staff meetings; the manager could have been a positive role model for you or inspired you to continue with your training.

Can you describe the most demanding problem you encountered in your last role? How did you solve it? As an example, you could talk about finding time management difficult and how you developed a strategy to deal with it.

Scenario-based questions

Working with children can be challenging: what is your approach in dealing with the more difficult children? You could say that all behaviour is communication and typically if a child is presenting with difficult behaviour they are communicating a need. You could use event sampling (ABC charts – antecedent, behaviour and consequences – from child development theory) to see if you could identify the trigger for the behaviour. Positive reinforcement is also an important tool in helping children manage their behaviour.

Parents can be difficult at times, especially when upset or dissatisfied. Is there a secret to placating them? Good communication is the key. It is also important to manage your body language and engage in active listening; to allow them the opportunity to explain why they are upset; and to manage the environment so that the discussion is not in front of the children or other parents. Active listening involves you repeating back to the parent what they are saying so that they know they have been heard. This also gives them the opportunity to calm down. It is very important not to be confrontational or defensive and to hear what the parent has to say.

Tell me about a time you had to deal with an angry child. De-escalation is a very important technique. You should explain that when a child is angry, listening to the child and managing the environment can be very important. Ideally you should be able to intervene before a child escalates to being angry, by redirecting or diverting the child.

Describe a highly stressful situation when you were able do your job in spite of the circumstances. Think about a challenge you have experienced and explain how you continued to do your job despite the highly stressful situation. An example might be dealing with an upset parent, as outlined above.

Describe a situation in which you alone had to make a quick decision and take immediate action. This question is aimed at seeing whether you can make decisions and work on your own initiative – a very important skill in childcare. If you have had to react quickly to a situation that could have been a health or safety issue you could outline that. An example would be stopping a child running onto the road or intervening when two children were having an argument, especially if there was physical aggression.

What experience have you had dealing with parents/guardians? Was there a situation you had to communicate under difficult circumstances? You could emphasise how important parents are when you are working with their children. Sometimes a supervisor in a childcare setting has to talk with parents when a child does not appear to be achieving the typical development milestones, for example. It is important that you never diagnose a condition but present factual observations. It is important to be empathetic and to present the information in a way that is clearly understood by the parents.

Can you describe your previous experience with students who have learning difficulties? If you have worked with a child with special needs you can outline your experience of this. If you have not worked with a child with a diagnosed special need, you could reflect on working with a child who presented with a particular need and outline how you supported that child.

If you were put in a position where you strongly disagreed with a particular teaching strategy that was being used, how would you deal with it? You should state that if there were an issue in relation to child protection you would challenge it and report it to the designated child protection officer in the ECCE service. If it were not a child protection issue, you should discuss the teaching strategy privately with the teacher/child care practitioner and discuss your concern about the strategy, outlining your concerns and listening to the teacher's rationale. You can always refer to your course tutor for advice here also.

Let us assume that you are working with younger students who are not fully toilet trained. How would you ensure their privacy while toilet training them? Refer to the policies and procedures in a childcare setting here – they outline what your practice should be. You could discuss how you use the toilets, how you can give verbal prompts, close a door but not lock it, and enable the child to do as much of the task as they can for themselves, positively reinforcing them with praise.

Explain how you would deal with challenging behaviour. Refer to de-escalation, redirection, diversion, ABC charts (as outlined above), positive reinforcement, managing the environment and so on. You should refer to your Child Development module for more guidance on how to deal with such questions.

These are only guidelines on how to answer interview questions. You should of course make sure that you answer any questions in an interview in a way that reflects your practice and understanding. The answers above are only one way of dealing with them. It is important to rehearse answering interview questions before the interview.

Sometimes at an interview you are asked if you have any questions you would like to ask. This can be an opportunity to show that you are interested in the ECCE setting. You could, for example, ask if they provide any additional training or about the curriculum in the service. Always leave the interview on a positive note; perhaps make a light joke if it is appropriate and the mood of the interview was right. Remember to shake hands, thank the interviewer(s) and ask when you will be notified if you are or are not successful.

JOB SEARCH SKILLS

If you are starting to look for a job there are a number of places where you can seek information, source potential jobs and get help with your search. If you are seeking a job in the childcare sector the resources below can get you started on seeking work in this area.

You may be looking for a job for when you complete your college course, or you may be thinking about changing jobs or returning to work. If you are unemployed, there are a number of services that can offer information and support to help you find a job. Whatever your situation, the process of finding and applying for a job is the same. It is very important to research all the potential sources of information regarding employment opportunities.

First identify the places where jobs are advertised; and regularly check all sources listed below to ensure that you are aware of any new vacancies.

▶ **Your local employment services office, Intreo**. Provides information and advice for jobseekers, including a list of job vacancies. Intreo is a new service from the Department of Social Protection (www.welfare.ie) that provides a single point of contact for all employment and income supports, including:

- ◆ expert assistance and advice on employment, training and personal development opportunities
- ◆ a focus on your individual needs
- ◆ self-service facilities to provide you with information and guidance on employment and training opportunities
- ◆ access to information on job vacancies through Jobs Ireland (www.jobsireland. ie); you can also upload your CV to the website, where it can be accessed by employers.

❱ **Websites:** Useful websites include:
- ◆ www.jobsireland.ie (see above)
- ◆ www.educationposts.ie – SNA posts are advertised here
- ◆ www.irishjobs.ie
- ◆ www.monster.ie
- ◆ www.twitter.com – #jobfairy, #jobfairyireland
- ◆ www.linkedin.com
- ◆ www.mychildcarejobs.ie – a dedicated childcare job site
- ◆ www.careerjet.ie – has a childcare section
- ◆ www.activelink.ie – social care jobs, some of which relate to childcare, are advertised here
- ◆ crèches' own websites or Facebook pages.

❱ **Newspapers:** There is typically a classified jobs section in national and local newspapers. Local papers, including free newspapers, are useful for finding jobs in your area.

❱ **Recruitment agencies:** Usually available online but will also be listed in the telephone directory. Recruitment agencies generally specialise in particular types of job.

❱ **Notices:** Jobs are often posted on noticeboards in shops, libraries, post offices, supermarkets, etc.

❱ **Companies:** Sometimes job vacancies are only advertised on a company website, so check those that might be relevant to you (e.g. www.barnardos.ie).

❱ **Personal contacts:** Friends or relations may know of job opportunities. One good reason for networking and keeping in touch with fellow classmates and tutors!

JOB-SEEKING TIPS

1. **Create a LinkedIn account and a Twitter account.** LinkedIn is like a professionals' version of Facebook. Jobs are advertised on LinkedIn, sometimes before or instead of being advertised on employment agency websites. Use Twitter to search for jobs using the hashtags #jobfairy and #irishjobfairy. Follow employment agencies, crèches and the @jobsfairy accounts. Install LinkedIn and Twitter on your smartphone (if you have one). This is a quick way to get job alerts direct to your phone. (See also Chapter 10 on using technology to find a job.)

2. **Ensure that your virtual/online presence is respectable** – most employers will search online for you. You may have heard of the term 'Google yourself'. This means typing your name into the Google search box and clicking on the search button to see what information is on the Internet about you. Try it now – you may be surprised by what you find. Be aware that employers could discover information that you would rather have kept private. If you have a Facebook profile, make it private. Don't post controversial messages on social media – these could offend your potential employer. Also think about the parents of the children you might work with – they may search for you too, and they probably would not be impressed if they found photos of you partying the night away.

3. **Sign up to employment agencies.** You can upload your CV to employment agency websites, which allows employers to see your CV. You will also get emails from the agency with potential jobs for you.

4. **Make your CV interactive.** If you have created Twitter and LinkedIn or any other social media accounts that you use in your job search, insert these details as hyperlinks in your CV. Insert hyperlinks to your college's and employer's websites in your CV. Many CVs are now emailed to agencies or employers and inserting hyperlinks will allow the potential employer to look more deeply at your CV.

5. **Create a Google Alert** for childcare jobs in your preferred location. You will receive an email whenever jobs are posted online or when jobs are announced.

6. **Check employment websites regularly.** Keep a record of the jobs that you have applied for. If you are applying for many jobs it is easy to become confused about what you have applied for and what you have not applied for.

7. **Email a copy of your CV and cover letter to yourself.** This way you can access them quickly and forward them on to potential employers. This will indicate that you are an organised person and that you are aware of how to take advantage of every opportunity that presents itself. You may find, through conversations with parents, friends, classmates, tutors and more, that they know of a job that may suit you. Applying on the spot can be vital if you only hear about a job just before the closing date.

8. **Be disciplined.** Update your CV regularly, even if you have found a job; this will keep your CV current and accurate. If you are asked to take on more responsibility in the workplace, add this to your CV immediately; if you leave it until later you might forget key facts.

9. **Update your LinkedIn profile** with new information too. Join LinkedIn groups relating to childcare. These groups will inspire you in your everyday job, act as a support mechanism if you are unsure about your role and identify key skills needed in the ever-changing workplace.

10. **Do not lie on your CV!** This may be tempting, especially if your CV is a little sparse at the beginning of your job hunting, but if a lie is detected you will not get the job!

If you are offered an interview ...

1. Think of answers to difficult interview questions; prepare as much as you can beforehand. Practise speaking your answers aloud or ask a friend to mock interview you.

2. If you can, find out before the interview how many people will be interviewing you. If there are two or more people, be sure to make eye contact with all of them.

3. Don't forget to smile! If you claim that your qualities include friendliness and fun, make sure this shines through. Try to forget your nerves; you got the interview, so you obviously have the skills they are looking for. Relax and listen to the questions.

4. Answer the question you are asked. Sometimes when we are nervous, we don't listen to the question. If you find yourself waffling, stop and ask for the question to be repeated.

5. When you are asked a question, don't launch straight into the answer; pause and think about the words you want to use, remember the answers you practised and then speak clearly, not too slowly and not too fast.

6. Ask questions at the end of the interview, for example when you should expect to hear if you have been successful, how and when staff are appraised, whether there is a probation period.

7. Shake hands and thank the interviewer(s) for the opportunity. Say that you are very interested in the role/job and would be grateful if they can seriously consider you. Reiterate that you are passionate about working in childcare and feel that you would be an effective employee.

8. Believe in yourself! If you do not believe that you are capable and would be a good person for the job, it will probably come across in the interview.

Being an Effective Employee

QUALITIES REQUIRED IN THE WORKING ENVIRONMENT

We have already seen in this book that certain personal skills are required for working in the early years sector. In addition to these there are other qualities which, for the purpose of learning, have been called value-added traits – which in effect means that they add value to your work and make you more likely to be employed and retained in the early years sector. Wallace and Masters (2006) state:

> There are three important keys for your success in the workplace. First is the technical knowledge and skills to do the job. (This is acquired through education and training.) Second is the ability and motivation to work effectively. (This comes from inside each individual.) Third is the personality that will allow you to fit in as a member of a working team.

Practice in an early years setting is guided by a number of legal requirements, regulations and guidelines. These include the Child Care Act 2001; the Childcare (Pre-School Services) (No 2) Regulations 2006; Síolta, the National Quality Framework; and Aistear, the Early Childhood Curriculum Framework (NCCA 2009a); the National Standards for Pre-School Services; and Children First (DCYA 2011).

All legal requirements, regulations and guidelines are available from the relevant websites (see pages 149–50 of this book).

All these regulations and guidelines focus on the importance of our practice in an ECCE setting and the qualities that are necessary to work effectively with children. There are specific personal traits and qualities that are valued in the early years setting and that will benefit the early years service where you are completing your work placement or are employed. You should think about whether you possess these qualities and whether you can develop or improve them. Remember, you do not need to be the most popular, interesting, entertaining and charismatic person to work successfully with children. You simply need some positive characteristics, such as being approachable and being kind, which children, parents and your co-workers will expect to see and will appreciate.

In order to do this effectively it helps if you are able to see things from the perspective of others; to see things from their point of view. This is an important skill when working with children and your demonstration of empathy will model good practice for the children you will be working with.

For example, let's look at someone who is applying for a position as a room supervisor in an ECCE service. There will be a number of different people who will have different expectations not only of what the role will be but also of the kind of person they would like to see fulfilling this role. So consideration needs to be given to the wants and needs of:

▶ the children

▶ the parents

▶ the service

▶ work colleagues/teammates.

An employer's view

Adrienne Jackson is the owner and manager of a crèche in north County Dublin. She runs a busy crèche with seven activity rooms and 14 staff members. Staff are employed under a number of contract types, including full time, part time, and on call or 'SOS'. Adrienne welcomes work experience students into her crèche and takes a proactive approach in helping them with their studies. At any one time, Adrienne will have six work experience students working within the service. Students come from different colleges, including institutes of technology, further education/post-leaving certificate courses, and transition year students from secondary schools.

When students ask to complete their work experience in Adrienne's crèche she invites them to visit the crèche so that she can spend some time getting to know the student, their needs and the details of the course they are completing and how they are expected to complete their work experience – in a single block, or one or a number of days per week. Adrienne brings the student on a tour of the crèche, explaining the different rooms, and introduces the student to the staff.

Adrienne is concerned with quality of service and experience, which extends to her staff and work experience students. She gives students a welcome pack containing the crèche's policies and procedures, guidelines on how to dress and a code of conduct. This is important as it makes it clear to the students what is expected of them.

Adrienne ensures that the needs of the work experience student are addressed and the week is planned with the student to enable them to complete observations and activities required for their coursework. Adrienne was once a student too and always remembers the kindness and support she received when she completed her own work experience. She strives to build a caring and learning environment for everyone who enters her crèche, whether a child, a parent, a member of staff or a student.

Adrienne has had good experiences with students who have worked in her crèche; however, she stresses that it is vitally important for a childcare practitioner to be reliable and punctual. She says that a student or employee who does not turn up for work can upset the children and the smooth running of the crèche. One staff member is known as her 'SOS' – someone she can always rely on to come in at the drop of a hat and cover for employees who are absent. Of course, staff can become ill or have to deal with sudden family crises and Adrienne understands this.

If there are continuing problems with any work experience student, Adrienne contacts the college directly and usually the student is relocated to another service, although this is a very rare event. Adrienne is honest when completing the supervisor's report during and at the end of the work experience because she believes that the student will otherwise not learn what skills and qualities they possess and what they must improve upon. She relates this to the quality of service provided for the children.

Adrienne states that it is important to role-model behaviour and she nurtures her work experience students to help them become confident childcare practitioners. Students are bound to be nervous for their first few days in a new environment and Adrienne waits patiently for them to gain confidence in their role and duties. Those students who ask lots of questions and intuitively get on the floor to play with the children stand out, according to Adrienne. She also highlights the important skill of being able to 'read a room', meaning an ability to see when children are too tired or too energetic to complete an activity, and to change a plan to suit the needs of the children.

Adrienne does not have to advertise for staff as many of her employees were once work experience students. This demonstrates the importance of being an effective student/employee – you might impress your supervisor/manager so much that you get a job! Due to economic issues Adrienne can't always offer the remuneration that she thinks her employees deserve, but she does reward them in different ways. She encourages her staff to further their education and development and will pay for them to complete FETAC Level 6 courses and other courses that they think can help them improve their practice. In these times of recession, the staff welcome this invaluable support. Not only are employees trained, but the service and, most important, the children in the service benefit from these perks. Adrienne also organises social evenings where staff receive awards for their work and efforts throughout the year. This is an opportunity to have fun with colleagues, relax and unwind and build a positive team rapport. At times, Adrienne will also bring staff on overnight stays in hotels to show how much she appreciates them. Lucky them!

Source: an interview with Adrienne Jackson, owner and manager of Funtimes Crèche, Balbriggan, Co. Dublin.

EMPLOYERS' EXPECTATIONS

Beginning a work experience placement can be a daunting task and it is important to know what is expected of you in the workplace and what you can expect from your employer.

Timekeeping and attendance

In a work environment, puncutality and good attendence are very important. It is particularly important in childcare settings, where specific child:adult ratios need to be maintained and where children come to rely on you being there. Attendance and punctuality is one of the simplest things to rate an employee on, if accurate time records are kept. It is something you need to be very aware of on your work placement.

Also remember that you role-model good timekeeping and attendance to the children you work with, and that children can be disrupted if your attendance or punctuality is poor. Research shows that children with poor timekeeping skills and poor school attendance are at a disadvantage later in life. They often find it harder to make and maintain friendships and are less likely to gain good qualifications. They also tend to earn lower wages and have a higher chance of being unemployed. Some children go on to have low self-esteem.

Poor attendance and punctuality, even at the earliest age, can affect achievement in later life. Establishing good habits from the start helps children to settle more quickly and the routine of regular attendance and good timekeeping will serve a child well for the rest of their school career and throughout their life. Regular attendance and good punctuality are also important for maximising achievement and accruing the greatest benefit from education.

You can help the children you work with by setting a good example yourself.

Personal presentation/approachability

In a work placement you create an impression by how you present yourself, the language you use, the way you greet the children and people that you work with. Are you approachable to the children and childcare staff you work with?

How you speak

Think about how you come across in the ECCE setting. Are you confident – or arrogant? Are you surly – or quiet and timid? The children need to hear you use your voice. Do you speak clearly or do you mumble? How we speak is very important and will be covered in more detail in Chapter 8 on communication.

What you say

Your choice of words is vital in an ECCE setting. Do not use slang and do not swear; remember that children learn from social modelling. Answer questions clearly and honestly and don't waffle. Be aware of what you're saying, who you're saying it to and therefore the message that might be conveyed. Sometimes it is how you say something, not what you say, that matters.

Body language

Be aware of the messages you are communicating by the way you stand, greet a person and generally hold yourself. You should make sure not to 'stand over' the children that you work with. Make eye contact with those you are talking to and use an appropriate tone of voice.

Clothes

Think carefully about what to wear in an ECCE setting. Many services provide a uniform, but if this is not supplied you need to dress smartly and in clothes that you can move in easily. Jewellery needs to be limited in a childcare setting for health and safety reasons.

Personal hygiene

It should go without saying that you must attend to your personal hygiene in any work setting, washing daily and ensuring that you wash your hands during nappy changes, food preparation, after toileting and so on.

Positive traits

Being good-humoured

Being in good humour is contagious. If one staff member is in a good mood the mood will be 'caught' by others, including the children, staff and parents. A cheerful atmosphere is a productive one and good humour begets good humour. This is why childcare services like to employ and retain people who are good humoured, and these people are often promoted because of this personality trait. The single trait of being good humoured will make your colleagues want to work with you and enjoy working with you. It will also have a very positive affect on the children you work with. Here's an example.

CASE STUDY

A harassed mother arrives at the service with her 3-year-old child. She has battled traffic and her child's mood and has managed to arrive at the service a few minutes early. Part of your remit is to welcome the children into the room each morning. You welcome both of them and say, 'It's so good to see you, Carl. Isn't it lovely to see the sun shining this morning after all the rain we have had? Did you tell Mam about how good you were yesterday and how hard you worked on your project?' Smiling, you lead both of them over to the interest table and show the parent the project Carl has been working on so well for the last few days. The mother leaves the service feeling much less stressed than she was when she arrived.

Discuss:

- the impact of what you did and said on both the mother and the child
- the effect on your colleagues in the room
- the effect on the reputation of the service.

A happy worker makes things less difficult. S/he dispels gloom, makes others happy, and looks on the brighter side of life. A good-humoured childcare practitioner energises others. In the example above, not only was the ripple effect extremely positive for all concerned, but you also contributed to some of the main themes of Aistear – under identity and belonging, and wellbeing – which can be viewed as a less tangible pieces of quality ECCE provision.

Sense of humour

Most people appreciate a good sense of humour; and many people consider that humour is necessary for mental, emotional, spiritual and physical well-being. A sense of humour is something you can cultivate if you feel that you are lacking a little in this trait. Laughter is without doubt the best medicine and, as long as it is not used at the expense of others or to hurt other people's feelings, it is an extremely positive contribution to the daily routine. Remember that laughter is a positive emotional release for all involved. Do not underestimate the positive impact that ripples throughout the whole service. A sense of humour can defuse potential conflict situations and de-escalate a child if they are getting upset or angry.

Discretion

Being discreet is the ability to do or say the right thing when dealing with difficult people or difficult situations. It includes diplomacy, the skill of maintaining good relations with others. Discretion involves understanding other people's needs and wishes. You may be a discreet person by nature, or you may need to practise being discreet. It is a skill you will need to use and perfect every day as you deal with parents, children, colleagues and management.

To take just one aspect of when this quality is of vital importance, part of your remit as an early years professional is to alert parents to any concerns regarding their child's holistic development. This is an extremely sensitive area for discussion and it requires discretion to handle it well. You will need to give a lot of thought to what you will say before approaching the parent(s).

You will need to avoid confrontational words, words that imply that you are pointing at the other person and confronting or blaming him or her; which will in turn make the other person feel challenged and become defensive.

Let's look at some guidelines that will help you learn how to exercise discretion. It can be helpful to look at the bigger picture; so, taking the example of a developmental issue with one of the children in the service, it might be useful to imagine what it would be like to be the parent of that child and to hear something that will have a big impact on both the parent and all the family members. Imagine that it is you hearing this information for the first time, with no previous idea or indication of what was coming; think about how you would like to be told and use this for the basis of your own discussion. Remember all the time how you would feel if it were your own child being discussed.

Parents can be defensive about their own children and their behaviour, and when you ask to speak to them they may jump to the conclusion that their child has behaved badly at the ECCE service, and so they may be defensive before you even begin to speak. It is always a good idea to begin with something positive followed by a general discussion around your concerns. Seek the parent's opinion to ascertain whether your concerns are valid, while also helping the parent feel included in the concerns rather than having to defend their child.

Finally, give serious consideration to the words and phrases you use. This is something which requires a lot of thought and perhaps discussions with more experienced colleagues, especially if you are on a work placement. Never underestimate the importance of discretion in this and other contexts in the workplace. If you feel that this type of scenario is something you are not yet ready to deal with, discuss the issue with your supervisor: not making them aware of it could only compound an already difficult situation.

Never respond immediately when a response requires discretion. Depending on the situation, it might be better to take some time out to consider what you are going to say. If you find that you are very angry and annoyed about someone's actions you might be better waiting until the next day before dealing with it. You are the one who knows yourself best, and based on this you need to make a call in determining how long you need before you are able to approach a person or deal with a situation, using all your skills to allow you to be as tactful as possible.

The very fact that you now have an increased awareness of this skill, of its importance in the workplace, and the impact of your responses on all parties involved, has set you on the right path to improving and consolidating this skill.

You may also receive confidential information about a child in your work placement; you must never disclose this information and you must exercise discretion in relation to it.

Empathy

Empathy is a quality or trait which is closely associated with discretion. Empathy is the ability to participate in another person's feelings or ideas, to understand and feel another person's emotions – to walk in another person's shoes. Empathy is not the same as pity, which is a negative trait. Pity, or feeling sorry for someone, is not empathy. When you pity someone you look down on them (whether intentionally or not); pity sets you apart while empathy brings you together – and therein lies the core difference.

Empathy really only comes from one's own life experiences. For example, the parent of a child with special needs will be able to feel empathy for another parent in a similar position.

If you can be sensitive to the feelings of others, you will be able to make them feel at ease and at the same time reassure them that you understand. Once again, we should not estimate the importance of allowing other people to feel at ease; this is an extremely important and valuable trait when working with young children and their families.

Each of us has experienced a variety of different problems and issues throughout our lives, and this in turn affects how we act, not only in the ECCE service but in all areas of our lives. Other people's displays of emotions or feelings may annoy or disturb you, but you must try and realise that there are reasons behind their actions.

Learning to react in an emotionally appropriate manner in the workplace to a variety of different situations and scenarios is something that will come not only from training and awareness but also with experience and length of time in your chosen career.

Childcare practitioners can have difficulty with empathy; while they are naturally caring, kind, responsive people – which is a must in order to be successful in this career – there can also be a tendency to respond to situations emotionally. The skill of learning to distance yourself in order to protect your own emotional well-being can take some time and a lot of hard work. However, as with the skill of discretion, an awareness that this is what will be needed in order to be successful sets you on the right path.

Liking children

It might seem obvious that you should have a genuine and natural affinity for children and are empathetic to their needs. You need to feel comfortable relating to children, enjoy spending time with them, and be motivated to help them. A positive, friendly attitude when you are around children is the most obvious sign of this trait. As described in the employer's case study at the beginning of this chapter, a childcare worker must be able to get on the ground with children and enjoy playing with them.

Patience

Patience is a core requirement for working in childcare. The children you work with will present with all kinds of issues and challenges, which can be stressful, frustrating and require your full attention. If children present with challenging behaviour or are upset, a childcare practitioner should be patient and calm enough to handle the situation effectively. You should present with a calm persona and an even temperament when dealing with such situations.

Communication skills

See also Chapter 8.

Being able to communicate with children clearly and in a positive way is an essential characteristic for a childcare practitioner. Children need you to explain things, give directions and direct their behaviour, as well as comfort them. A childcare practitioner also has to communicate with parents or co-workers, sharing information to show that the child is progressing and is being well cared for. Childcare practitioners may have to complete Aistear observations, write progress reports, or contribute to assessments for children, all of which requires good written communication skills.

Energy
When you work with children you are not going to be able to sit down all day! You need to be very active in this job. Children tend to have a lot of energy and trying to keep up with them is part of your role as a childcare practitioner. You need to be constantly alert and focused and good energy levels are required for this. Taking care of your health is one way to ensure you have enough energy. Make sure that you take your allotted breaks, eat and drink at regular intervals throughout the day. If you are not taking care of yourself, this will affect your mood, which will in turn affect the children in your care.

Training
In a childcare setting it is important to have trained practitioners in areas such as first aid, manual handling, HACCP (food hygiene) as well as the FETAC Early Childcare and Education Awards or a degree programme in childcare.

Negative trait

Resentment
This is a common negative trait that needs to be avoided, whatever your chosen career. Resentment is a feeling of displeasure over something you believe (correctly or incorrectly) to be a wrong, insult, slight or injury. When openly expressed, resentment comes across as grumbling and complaining. People who grumble and complain because they resent others, the workplace, or a specific situation are not pleasant people to be around. More often than not the grumbler finds themselves alone and excluded by colleagues. Earlier we spoke about good humour being contagious and the benefits of this; unfortunately, resentment is also contagious and this can have a detrimental effect on both colleagues and the childcare service itself. If you exhibit

resentment, the only person who can change this aspect of your personality is yourself; and it will take a lot of hard work both to be aware that you are moaning and to break that habit to set you on track. This is something that perhaps could be looked at in terms of goals and what is realistic to expect of yourself to achieve within a given timeframe. When you look at things through a negative lens you tend to see negativity. Try to focus on the positives and this should help you reframe how you come across in your work placement.

All your traits or characteristics inform how you present and behave in your childcare work placement. You need to be aware of your own strengths and of areas that need to be developed. Chapter 5 on reflection should support you in developing self-awareness, and the sections on goal setting and skills audits should support you in auditing the skills you have and that you need to develop.

EMPLOYEE/STUDENT EXPECTATIONS

When beginning a work placement or job, employees should expect to be treated fairly and with respect, regardless of qualifications and experience. Employees should expect to work in an environment that is safe for them and the children they are in charge of. Employees are entitled by law to take allotted breaks, depending on the number of hours they work in a day.

Employees should expect to gain recognition for work well done, if not every day, at least at special occasions throughout the year. It is usual to have an annual appraisal where the employer meets with the employee to discuss their performance and to identify any areas they would like to improve upon. This is a chance for both parties to air any grievances they may have and to put in place a positive plan for tackling any challenges the employee is facing. Outcomes of appraisals should usually involve statements of recognition of work well done, offers of training if needed and asked for, and/or bonuses and pay rises (although these are not always possible, especially in today's economy).

THE ROLE OF THE COLLEGE SUPERVISOR

The college supervisor is charged with making sure that the student on work placement is gaining as much experience on the job as possible. They should ensure that the student feels supported by the college and they must alert the employer to any concerns they may have about the work experience placement. For example, it is not good practice to leave work experience students supervising a room because they are not experienced enough, and they may not have the necessary qualifications. If this happens, the student should inform their tutor, who should then contact the employer to pass on the student's concerns. This can be a difficult situation to deal with for all involved and tact and diplomacy are required.

Colleges sometimes provide a letter to the student to give to their work placement, in which they outline the requirements of the work placement. It is important for the student to learn to communicate any concerns or issues with the employer directly and not to rely too much on the tutor. Tutors may also visit the work placement to listen to any concerns the employer may have about the suitability of the student to work in the childcare sector.

Activity

Discuss with your tutor the expectations of the employer, the employee and the college before you go to your work placement. What documentation do you need from the college to successfully complete your placement? What are your concerns about beginning your work placement? Are you aware of the legal aspects of work experience? If not, clarify this with your college before going out to the workplace.

Communication

Communicating involves giving, receiving and making sense of information. We do this by using both verbal and non-verbal means of communication. Verbal communication involves talking, and the written word. Non-verbal communication involves symbols, gestures, tone of voice, body language and expressions.

Young children typically use gestures to communicate their needs. Gestures can be easier to understand than other forms of non-verbal communication.

Examples of a child using non-verbal communication:

- pointing to a drink
- raising their arms to be picked up
- shaking their head to say yes or no
- waving
- blowing a kiss.

In these examples, the intent is clear. When the child learns to speak and write it enhances the experience of communication.

Communicating is a two-way activity; it is not just about sharing experiences but how to interpret information and making sure that the message is both given and received. The sender sends a message, the receiver gets the message and then the receiver sends another message – the feedback – back to the sender and the process starts all over again.

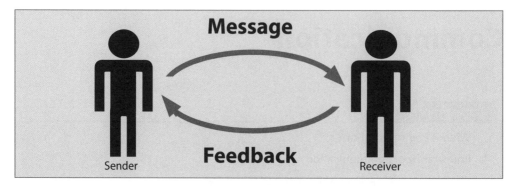

We use both verbal and non-verbal communication to communicate.

- Verbal communication: spoken and written words.
- Non-verbal communication: gestures, sign language, tone of voice, the way you hold your body, proximity, your use of facial expressions to convey meaning.

The three basic elements of communication – sender, receiver and message – are combined into two basic patterns for communication: one-way communication; and two-way communication.

▶ **One-way communication.** The sender transmits a message, the receiver gets it and the process is complete. For example, when your tutor gives you the next assignment, you write it down and leave the classroom, this is one-way communication. An example in the workplace is putting a notice on a noticeboard. This is appropriate in some circumstances – for instance if you are telling parents about the week's theme or an upcoming coffee morning – but generally the childcare practitioner should try to maximise methods that encourage two-way communication and feedback to ensure that the message has been received.

▶ **Two-way communication.** The sender transmits a message, the receiver receives it, and then the receiver responds with another message as outlined in the diagram above. Conversations are an obvious example. Two-way communication is seen as the most effective form of communication, particularly when there is direct face-to-face communication, as the sender can get an immediate reaction, both the verbal reply and also the receiver's body language.

Successful communication is an exchange of messages that are understood by both the sender and receiver; both sender and receiver have the same understanding of the message.

When a baby or child initiates communication with you, such as by crying or grabbing your hand or making eye contact, how you respond helps the child to learn to communicate.

The child learns that:

▶ what they have to communicate is important

▶ you are taking the time to listen to them

▶ turn-taking is a core requirement for speech

▶ communication is two-way – they communicate, you reply and they respond.

A child's attempt to communicate can be sometimes very subtle.

CASE STUDY

Jane was sitting beside the childcare practitioner and they were doing an art activity. Jane was gluing coloured shapes on a card. She ran out of sparkly circles and asked the childcare practitioner for some more, pointing to the circles she wanted, but she had no response from the childcare worker. A few minutes later she gestured to the circles again, but no one noticed. She then started to bang on the table and was told to stop banging on the table or she would be asked to leave the activity. Having had no positive response to her many requests, Jane was very upset when she left the art table.

This example shows what can happen when you do not respond to a child initiating communication. If Jane had been able to speak and use words to ask for the sparkly shapes the situation would not have ended so negatively. Even though Jane had used her communication skills, they were not responded to.

When you work with groups of young children, it can be hard to respond to each child's request or attempt to communicate. In your work placement it is important to be aware of a child's communication and that the children you work with feel that their contribution is welcome and encouraged.

You should acknowledge each child, making sure to include the child who might be quiet or less competent in communication. Use your observation skills to notice a gesture or comment from the children who are less able to contribute, particularly during group activities. Try not to miss the opportunity to encourage good communication skills with each child you work with in your work placement.

Communicating is in a general sense about people sharing their experiences, thoughts, ideas and feelings with others – and about the message being understood.

This means that in an ECCE setting the children you work with, the parents, your co-workers and your supervisor all need to communicate effectively with each other.

Communication can happen in many different ways, including facial expressions, gestures, body movements, sounds, language and, for some people, through assistive technology.

Communication in an ECCE setting is so important that it is one of the four themes in Aistear:

> The ability to communicate is at the heart of early learning and development. Communication helps children learn to think about and make sense of their world. They communicate from birth using many different ways of giving and receiving information. Each of these ways is important in its own right. Learning to communicate in early childhood is shaped by two main factors: children's own ability and their environment. (NCCA 2009a:12)

Being a good communicator in an ECCE setting is an essential skill.

THE IMPORTANCE OF GOOD COMMUNICATION IN AN ECCE SETTING

Good communication is very important because it can:
▪ motivate the children, parents and the other people you work with
▪ facilitate decision-making
▪ improve relationships with the children, parents and co-workers
▪ enable relationship-building with the children you work with
▪ demonstrate an interest in what the child is doing
▪ help children learn to follow direction
▪ help scaffold learning.

Communication is a core requirement in an ECCE setting. Standard 12 of Síolta outlines that:

> Communicating effectively in the best interests of the child requires policies, procedures and actions that promote the proactive sharing of knowledge and information among appropriate stakeholders, with respect and confidentiality.

Parents and those who care for a baby wait anxiously for the child to speak their first words and are delighted by the child's efforts to communicate their needs. But before those first words appear the children we work with are already able to express themselves. A young baby learns to communicate, moving from a reflexive cry to a directed cry, within the first three weeks of life. At six months the baby is able to effectively communicate a need, through:

- crying
- grimacing
- smiling
- pouting
- laughing
- frowning
- gesturing

- making faces
- babbling
- screaming
- rubbing eyes
- kicking
- arching their back
- widening their eyes

The baby also moves their arms and legs to communicate a message. Facial expressions are one of the earliest expressions of a child's need. When a young child cries or catches hold of your arm or leg the parent/childcare practitioner typically knows what the child is trying to communicate, even though they may not have used any actual words. Babies and toddlers use strategies such as crying, smiling, laughing, gestures, movement, screaming and babbling to communicate, as outlined above.

A child in your work placement may make eye contact with you as a way to initiate interaction. Some children you work with may have disabilities that inhibit their ability to communicate with you and they rely on non-verbal communication, such as facial expressions, to communicate a need and to engage in social interaction.

As the baby grows into a child they learn to speak, listen, turn-take and to read and write, so their communication improves. We encourage children 'to use their words' to communicate emotions and feelings.

As a child grows and develops it is very important to support their communication, especially for children with English as a second language or those who present with a language difficulty/disability.

COMMUNICATION SKILLS IN AN ECCE SETTING

Most of us have developed our communication skills without actually giving much thought to them and how they developed, but in a working environment with children it is very important that we consider how we communicate and what we communicate.

The role of the early childhood practitioner in promoting effective communication in an ECCE setting is very important. You can promote a child's communication in a work placement by encouraging a child or the children you work with to practise their communication skills through play, songs, stories, role play and by talking to the child as you engage with their care and education routines, which thus become enriching communication opportunities.

Children benefit from being in an ECCE setting where the environment promotes both non-verbal and verbal communication. Putting a picture of a jigsaw where the jigsaws are kept helps the child to understand what you mean when you ask them to get the jigsaw. Using dolls, teddies, story bags, story boards and puppets gives children the opportunity to use both non-verbal and language-based information to understand, enjoy and learn.

When a childcare practitioner gets to know the children they work with, they can typically learn to distinguish between the cries and gestures of different children, as well as correctly understanding what a child is trying to communicate.

All children can communicate, even if they are just using their eyes or eye contact, gestures, smiling, pointing, or one word: all these can express what a child is interested in or if they want something in particular or have a specific need.

A child can also communicate how they feel about something by their physical pose. How they position themselves in relation to an activity, person or object communicates how they feel about it. A child who moves away from something or someone is usually showing that they are uncomfortable with it in a certain way, and they may move toward a familiar adult to gain comfort. When children feel secure and comfortable in the ECCE setting, they will be more likely to join in play activities.

EFFECTIVE COMMUNICATION

There are a number of factors that facilitate effective communication.

▶ Think about the language you use. Is it age- and stage-appropriate?

▶ Consider how fast you talk: you may need to speak a little slower.

▶ Give appropriate feedback and praise.

▶ Be specific when you ask the child to do something. Don't use non-specific direction such as 'be good' – a child may not know what you mean by 'being good'.

▶ Make eye contact with the child, get down to their level.

▶ Use visual displays for children who do not speak English as their first language.

▶ Use picture exchange communication systems (PECS), examined below.

▶ Use Lámh – a shortened version of sign language – for children with autism or intellectual disability.

▶ Help develop children's emotional intelligence by using words to express their feelings.

Communication is about the different ways in which people relate their feelings, ideas and concepts and it is not something that we should take for granted. In an ECCE setting there may be children who present with communication challenges such as a difficulty forming words, a stammer, a lisp or difficulty speaking. The children might have problems understanding what you say to them or what you are asking them to do. In order to respond to children's communication needs, you should know what the child's baseline is in relation to their current language skills and the typical milestones for language development (Flood 2013).

Communication with children should be framed positively: ask the child to do something rather than telling them not to do something. A childcare practitioner should use positive statements, such as 'Let's be nice to our friends' rather than 'Give that car back to Jack.' If an adult says to a child, 'Don't run out to the car!' it appears as if the child does not hear the 'Don't' and is in fact encouraged to engage in the inappropriate behaviour.

Aistear asks the childcare practitioner to consider communication from the child's perspective:

> You have a key role in supporting my communication and language skills. Talk to me, listen to me, respond to me, interpret what I say, and provide a place for me where I get the opportunity to share my experiences, thoughts, ideas, and feelings with others in all the ways that I can. Model communication and language skills for me. (NCCA 2009a)

BARRIERS TO COMMUNICATION

There are a number of barriers to effective communication in an ECCE setting:

▶ The noise levels can be such that the message simply cannot be heard!

▶ If you are distracted you may not notice a child trying to communicate, especially if they are using non-verbal cues.

▶ Not allowing the child to say what they want to say, instead finishing the sentence for them.

▶ Using vocabulary that is not suitable for the particular age/stage of the child.

▶ Poor hearing – this can be transient, for example when you have a cold.

▶ Beta commands – non-specific instructions such as 'pay attention', when you do not say specifically what you want the child to attend to.

PICTURES IN COMMUNICATION

Pictures are widely used to support communication in an ECCE setting. A child's photo is placed beside where they hang their coat and pictures are used to label boxes. Pictures of different activities can be used in timetables, for example a picture of a cup and plate for break time or a paint brush for art time. Pictures can be laminated and Velcro attached to the back, and these pictures can then be placed on a felt board and the child, with the ECCE practitioner, can then create their own activity list. Pictures can be used to support verbal communication, and for some children who are non-verbal they can be used as an effective means of communication in themselves.

Picture exchange communication system (PECS)

PECS is a form of augmentative communication where pictures are used to communicate with a child in a two-way process. The system is best known as a communication aid for children with autism spectrum disorder, but it is also used in pre-school settings for children with a variety of communicative, cognitive and physical disabilities. The goal of PECS is to initiate spontaneous and functional communication.

PECS starts by teaching a child to exchange a picture of a desired item with a childcare practitioner, who immediately complies with the request. A reinforcer is used to promote the communication and the reinforcer used must be something that is meaningful for the child, for example a preferred activity, a toy the child likes to play with, or food.

COMMUNICATION WITH PARENTS

Effective communication is very important in an ECCE setting. You may not have much opportunity to communicate with parents in your work placement – this will depend on where you are working and what your role is – but it is important to get to know the parents and to use their preferred name, rather than referring to them as 'Jake's mum' or Katie's dad'.

Standard 3 of Síolta states:

> Valuing and involving parents and families requires a proactive partnership approach evidenced by a range of clearly stated, accessible and implemented processes, policies and procedures. (CECDE 2006)

We should consider what a partnership approach involves when we are communicating with parents in our work practice. Good communication with parents helps early childhood practitioners understand what is happening at home and how the parents would like their children's behaviour managed in the service.

Barriers to effective communication with parents can include:
- communicating with a parent who does not have English as their first language
- being too busy, especially at drop-off and collection times
- meetings being scheduled during the day when most parents are working
- childcare workers being dismissive of what the parent says (sometimes demonstrated with body language more than words).

If childcare practitioners communicate effectively with parents there will be a clear understanding of what the child is doing in the ECCE setting and how they are getting on.

Communication with parents can be **promoted** by:
- relationship building between parents and the ECCE service
- a handbook that outlines what a parent can expect from the service
- giving meaningful feedback to parents about their child
- sharing information and observations
- showing parents that they are listened to
- having an open door policy
- face-to-face meetings
- phone calls (which should, however, be avoided if a parent is learning English)
- newsletters
- communication book to link the home and the ECCE setting
- a service website
- noticeboard at the entrance to the service displaying news, themes, menu, etc.

Remember that non-verbal communication is less direct than verbal communication. We can usually observe what people mean from their body language (e.g. if they lean towards you or they cross their arms), gestures, facial expression and tone of voice.

We often rely more on non-verbal communication to communicate a message than the words we use. For example, if someone asks you how you are you might say 'I'M FINE', emphasising with your body language and tone of voice that you are not actually 'fine'. So your body language belies what you are saying.

> Have you ever met someone and thought that maybe they are uncomfortable around you? They might not say anything, but their body language communicates how they really feel about you.

TECHNOLOGY AND COMMUNICATION

The development of technology has influenced the way we communicate today. For example, while the fax machine was a popular form of communication for businesses in the 1980s, it is very seldom used these days; people largely use email, text messaging and social media instead.

When using technology to communicate, general communication rules must be followed: when the communication is work-related matter, don't swear in emails or texts, don't share inappropriate images, jokes or gossip.

It is best not to use 'textspeak' abbreviations in text messages (for example 'TTYL' for 'talk to you later') just in case the receiver does not understand what they mean. Don't use capital letters in texts as this can be interpreted as shouting. Using emoticons such as a smiley face :-) can help express an emotion in a text message. They shouldn't be overdone, but they can be useful to show the meaning behind a text message, which can sometimes be misconstrued. Smartphones, including iPhones, often replace words in text messages, so it is important to double-check the message before hitting the Send button. Sometimes words are unintentionally replaced with rude or offensive words, so be careful!

Social media applications such as Twitter, Facebook, Pinterest and Blogger can be used to inform parents of the daily activities in a childcare setting. Private Facebook pages can be set up for use by each room in a setting or for the whole facility. Parents can be invited to become 'friends' of the page, enabling them to see photos and updates. It is advisable that parents sign release or consent forms, as not all parents will be happy with this arrangement; or, for more confidential communication, you could email photos to parents. Photos can also be shared via Twitter or on a Pinterest board. Blogger, which is a free online blogging tool, could be used to write about the activities planned for the day, show photos and videos, communicate information, inform parents of planned day trips and more.

All these tools will help parents feel that they are involved in their children's day, which is very important. If parents use the tools to communicate with you and other parents you are creating a community around the child.

The internet is a key tool for many ECCE settings to communicate. Some have cameras linked to the internet so that parents can see their child in the ECCE setting from their workplace. Some ECCE settings also use the internet for advertising, to display the children's work and communicate their news.

> Why not visit these social media pages and see how they might be used for communication?
> - www.facebook.com
> - www.pinterest.com
> - www.twitter.com
> - www.blogger.com

CULTURE AND COMMUNICATION

Diversity refers to differences between individuals, for example in family circumstances, family values, language, religion or culture. Effective communication can help us to understand, respect and acknowledge diversity. Good communication needs to be supported to enable parents and the ECCE setting to share information, understand cultural norms and respect religious requirements.

Childcare practitioners need to understand what is important to families. The ECCE service should find out how parents would like to be informed about their child's day. Some parents prefer written communication, by email for example. If English is not their first language, they can use communication tools such as Google Translate or ask an English-speaking friend to read the communication. Other parents prefer face-to-face communication, in which they can pick up the non-verbal communication cues such as body language; but it should be borne in mind that there can be problems with non-verbal as well as verbal communication: body language can mean different things in different cultures. For example, making eye contact, shaking hands or using a person's first name can have different meanings in different cultures.

Pictures can help communication: make notices strongly visual and use pictures to support the written message. Most families will typically find that a combination of communication methods best meets their needs.

It can take time for families to be comfortable and friendly with other families and the ECCE setting. An ECCE setting should reflect the cultural backgrounds of all the children attending the setting and their families. This communicates respect. Since parents are the most knowledgeable about their own background, culture, language and needs, you should ask them what they would like to see in the ECCE setting. Find out how they would like their own culture, religions or traditions depicted and celebrated in the ECCE setting.

COMMUNICATION WITH COLLEAGUES

Good communication with your supervisor and the childcare workers in the ECCE setting is vital.

A supervisor's role is to support you in your work placement. Supervisors are responsible for providing childcare students with constructive feedback about their performance and how they interact with the children in an ECCE work placement. The supervisor has to evaluate your performance (see Chapter 7) and they should give you clear feedback that reflects how you have engaged in your work placement. Be sure to speak to your supervisor if you are unsure about what to do, or how to handle a situation. Make yourself familiar with the routines of the service, and learn to work on your own initiative – with the guidance and support of the childcare practitioners at your placement.

Formal communication occurs when staff in the ECCE setting use channels of communication that have been formally established by the setting, for example organised staff meetings and appraisals.

LISTENING

Listening is a very important skill that is used all the time in an effective ECCE setting. However, it is not always acknowledged as an important skill to develop in the children we work with. We praise children when they complete a picture or an activity, but we do not often say to the child, 'Good listening.' Through listening children develop their language skills and their ability to communicate. You can develop good listening skills with the children you work with by:

▶   reading them interesting stories

▶   making eye contact with them before you communicate with them

▶   using songs and music

▶   encouraging them to give and follow simple instructions and directions

▶   encouraging them to ask and answer questions

▶   teaching them to listen and turn-take in conversation

- asking open-ended questions, such as 'Tell me about your picture'
- exposing them to new words
- finding out a child's interest and letting them tell you about it
- talking with them, not at them
- when telling them a story, asking them to predict what might happen on the next page.

Listening is not just an important skill for the children you work with to learn; it is a core requirement for an ECCE practitioner in their everyday practice. Make sure that you pay attention when someone is speaking to you and that you listen without interrupting. Children and adults are very aware if someone they are speaking to is not fully paying attention or is only partly listening.

You are aware when someone is not listening to you if:

- they don't make eye contact
- they are staring into space
- they interrupt you before you have finished
- they don't stop what they are doing to give you their full attention
- they yawn or are evidently distracted and not paying attention.

Active listening

Active listening is a technique that helps you to be a better communicator. A childcare practitioner needs to be approachable and to listen carefully, paying attention to what the child is saying and doing. Listening actively to the children you work with is very important. Active listening involves being empathic and understanding things from the child's perspective. It involves seeing the situation as the child sees it and appreciating their feelings. An important strategy in active listening is to repeat back in the child's own words what they have said to you. This confirms for the child that you have heard them. For example, 'So Jack took the car from you and you had it first?' You are letting the child know that you understand what they are communicating to you and that you are going to respond to how they are feeling in an appropriate way. Active listening is respectful of the child; it identifies and expresses their emotions and assists the child to 'use their words' rather than to act out what they want to communicate.

Active listening is about:

- being respectful of the child and what they have to say
- being empathic
- acknowledging the child's feelings

▶ identifying and expressing the child's emotions

▶ helping the child to use their words rather than acting out

▶ repeating what the child has said to check you have understood and to let them know that they have been heard

▶ paying full attention and making eye contact

▶ encouraging communication by nodding, being silent, and asking appropriate questions.

These active listening skills apply not only to your engagement with the children; they can be very useful in your work placement in general. Letting people know that you value them, that you hear what they say, that you are listening and that they have been heard are all very important for developing your skills in your work experience. Repeating back to your supervisor what they asked you to do lets them know that you understand and clarifies for you what you are being asked to do. For example, the supervisor says, 'Can you get the children ready for outdoor play? They are going out in five minutes, and they need coats, hats, gloves and wellies.' You say to the supervisor, 'I'll organise the coats, hats, gloves and wellies and be ready in five minutes.'

BEHAVIOUR MANAGEMENT AND THE ECCE SETTING

A number of behaviour management strategies are used in an ECCE setting. Make sure that you follow the service's policies, procedures and protocols in relation to managing children's behaviour.

We tend to refer to difficult behaviour as 'challenging', although the word 'challenging' is not in itself a negative term. Children can present with a number of behaviours which can be disruptive or negative and we need to support the children we work with in how to manage behaviour.

We need to consider the role of positive reinforcement in promoting positive behaviour.

Positive reinforcement

Positive reinforcement is a concept first described by psychologist B. F. Skinner in his theory of operant conditioning. Positive reinforcement is anything added that follows a behaviour that makes it more likely that the behaviour will occur again in the future. (http://psychology.about.com)

Positive reinforcement means finding the opportunity to reinforce a child when they are engaged in an activity or task that is what you want them to do. You need to be proactive to 'catch them when they are being good' and to positively affirm that behaviour with an appropriate reinforcer.

It is also an incentive given to a child who complies with a request for behaviour change. The aim of positive reinforcement is to increase the chances that the child will respond with the changed behaviour. Positive reinforcement is given immediately after the desired behaviour has occurred so that it will shape the child's future behaviour.

When you work with children, you need to understand that different reinforcers can be effective with different children. You need to observe the child to see what their natural likes and dislikes are and this will help you to decide which reinforcer would be most effective.

There are a number of different types of reinforcer:

▶ **Natural reinforcement** results directly from the appropriate behaviour. A child finds that other children want to play with them when they are nice and they will want the other children to play with them again.

▶ **Social reinforcers:** praise and comments such as, 'Well done – you are working really hard' or 'Good listening!', or giving a child a high five are all social reinforcers. It is very important that the praise is based on real achievement or effort, otherwise it becomes meaningless.

▶ **Activity reinforcers**, where children get the opportunity to take part in a preferred activity. This can be referred to as 'Golden Time', when the child picks the activity they would like to do. These reinforcers are very effective.

▶ **Tangible reinforcers** include edibles, toys, balloons, stickers and awards. Edibles and toys should be used with caution. Children typically respond very well to stickers.

▶ **Token reinforcement** involves awarding points or tokens for appropriate behaviour. These rewards have little value in themselves but can be exchanged for something of value. For example, stickers can be used to fill a star chart, and when the required number are collected they can be exchanged for something meaningful for the child.

Reinforcements should be consistently delivered, according to a planned reinforcement schedule. If it is not, the child will not make the connection between the appropriate behaviour and the reinforcement and the behaviour will not change. Reinforcement should be delivered immediately. Reinforcements should be age-appropriate.

Other behaviour management strategies

Children tend to seek attention and if they have learned that they get attention from challenging behaviours, this achieves their goal of getting your attention. A child who is not getting positive attention will seek out negative attention – which is better for them than no attention at all. All behaviour is communication and the child might be expressing a need for attention that is not being met otherwise in the childcare setting.

Other behaviour management strategies you could use in an ECCE setting are:

▶ **Redirection:** If you see a child heading for trouble, redirect them to a more positive activity or place in the room.

▶ **Distraction:** Children can be distracted from negative behaviour with a new activity or by your attention.

▶ **Proximity:** Being close to the child can be calming – simply move close to the child who needs support and this can defuse a situation.

▶ **Scaffolding:** Support a child with new learning, especially if they appear to be frustrated, by a verbal prompt or by modelling what they have to do.

▶ **Environment:** Be aware of the impact the environment can have on children's behaviour, for example noise, adult interactions, physical space, sitting still for long periods, toys and the ECCE routine.

▶ **Clear, consistent guidance:** Give the children clear guidance that is consistent and framed positively, for example 'Please walk' rather than 'Don't run.'

▶ **Circle time:** Can be used to discuss issues and to solve problems.

▶ **Establish rules or 'happy habits':** Involve the children in developing the rules – which should be framed positively and state what you want the children to do. There should be around four to five rules in an ECCE setting.

These strategies are guidance for a more detailed discussion on managing behaviour in an ECCE setting: see Flood (2013).

CONFLICT RESOLUTION

Tensions can emerge in any workplace. It is very important that these are dealt with effectively and respectfully – and good communication skills help to do this. Active listening, which, as outlined earlier, is vital in working with children, can also be a very useful tool in situations of conflict. Allow the other person the time and space to say what they want to say and reframe their words so that they know that you have heard them.

In any setting, different people can see things in very different ways and have different perspectives; we need to understand that our perspective is not necessarily the only way or the 'right way' to understand the issue.

It is important to consider not just what we say but how we say it. When you want someone to do something, you could tell them in a dictatorial manner, or you could ask them, 'Would you mind doing ...?' – two very different approaches to what is generally the same outcome; the person doing what you need them to do.

Problem-solving skills can be useful in a situation of ongoing conflict. There are a number of steps involved in the problem-solving process:

▶ Identify what the conflict is about.

▶ Consider alternative solutions (you could seek advice here).

▶ Evaluate the possible solutions and decide which solution is best.

▶ Implement your preferred solution.

▶ After a period of time, evaluate the solution and determine whether it is working.

You should seek guidance and support from your course tutor if you find that you are in a conflict situation in your work placement. If possible, situations around conflict should be dealt with informally by using the problem-solving steps above. If this does not work, a decision must be made whether to arrange a formal meeting to resolve the issue, or whether an informal conversation or informal meeting would be best.

An informal meeting in which the parties involved in the conflict get together should be adequate to deal with most issues of conflict. The supervisor of the childcare setting can act as a facilitator, and the focus should be on reaching a mutual solution based on shared information and respect.

Information on how to make a formal complaint should be available if needed.

Your ECCE service will have a policy on how to deal with issues of conflict in the workplace and it should make you aware of the informal and formal processes for dealing with conflict issues that are in place in the service.

CHAPTER NINE

Further Education, Training and Career Opportunities

In this chapter

- Understanding FETAC and the NFQ framework
- Occupational profiles
- Childcare sector jobs

If you are a student studying at Level 5 or Level 6 you should be aware of the training and career opportunities that might be open to you. Over the past 20 years there have been many changes in the early years care and education sector in Ireland and as a result many different training and career opportunities are now available to students. Whether you have elected to do your training full time over one year or part time over two years or module by module, you will have invested a lot of time and energy in completing your certificate course. Therefore it is important that you have some idea of the training and progression paths within the sector.

In order to understand progression in education and what that means we need to look first at the FETAC 10 Level Framework.

The National Framework of Qualifications (NFQ) is intended to put you, the learner, at the centre of the education and training system in Ireland. The NFQ is used to classify and compare qualifications. This means that you can use the NFQ to find out more about courses you are interested in and to help you make informed decisions when choosing a course. The NFQ also makes it easier for you to explain to others what qualifications you hold or are studying for; this becomes very important when you are considering further learning or when you are applying for a job – at home or abroad. (National Framework of Qualifications (NFQ), www.nfq.ie)

For further information see www.nfq.ie and www.qqi.ie.

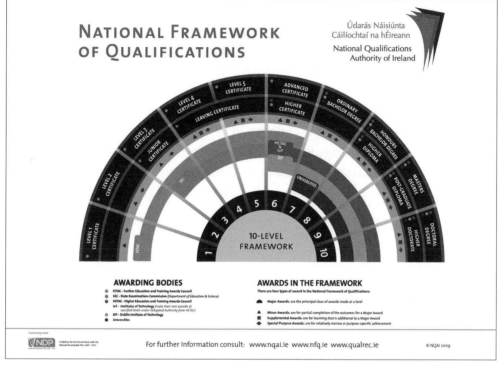

Each of the levels in the framework represents different levels of learning.

▶ **Levels 1 and 2:** a number of components, many in basic literacy and numeracy.

▶ **Level 3:** specific personal skills, practical skills and knowledge. This level is equivalent to the Junior Certificate programme in second-level schools.

▶ **Level 4:** vocational and personal skills. This award may lead to progression to a Level 5 certificate programme and employment at an introductory vocational level. Level 4 is equivalent to the Leaving Certificate programme in second-level schools.

▶ **Level 5:** a broad range of skills, which are vocation-specific and require a general understanding of the subject matter. The majority of certificate/module holders at Level 5 take up positions of employment. Holders of certificates at this level also meet the minimum entry requirements for a range of higher education programmes.

▶ **Level 6:** development of a range of skills which may be vocation-specific and/or of a general supervisory nature. The majority of Level 6 holders take up positions of employment. A Level 6 certificate holder may also transfer to a programme leading to the next level of the framework.

▶ **Level 7:** ordinary bachelor's degree after a three-year programme at a recognised higher education institution. Progression routes include an honours bachelor's degree or a Higher Diploma.

- **Level 8:** honours bachelor's degree or Higher Diploma following a one-year programme at a recognised higher education institution.
- **Level 9:** master's degree or a Postgraduate Diploma. Entry to a master's degree programme leading is typically restricted to holders of an honours bachelor's degree, but in some cases entry to such programmes can be permitted for those with ordinary first degrees. Holders of a Level 9 qualification could progress to a doctoral degree, another master's degree or a Postgraduate Diploma.
- **Level 10:** doctoral degree (e.g. PhD). There are various types of doctoral degree programme, from the traditional research doctorate to professional and practitioner doctoral programmes with substantial taught components.

Source: adapted from www.nfq.ie/nfq/en/about_NFQ/framework_levels_award_types.html (accessed 31 October 2013).

The NFQ is designed around Ireland's formal education system, which has been in existence for many years. When adult education came to the fore the different 'levels' were placed on a 'wheel' to help adult students equate their training and courses within the recognised training framework. All the levels, regardless of the vocational topic, are based on the literacy level needed to achieve the award.

EXPLAINING THE NFQ

Quality and Qualifications Ireland (QQI) was established as a new integrated agency in November 2012. It replaced the Further Education and Training Awards Council (FETAC), the Higher Education and Training Awards Council (HETAC) and the National Qualifications Authority of Ireland (NQAI) and it incorporates the functions of the Irish Universities Quality Board (IUQB). QQI has the responsibility for the external quality assurance of further and higher education and training and it also validates programmes and makes awards for certain providers in these sectors. QQI is also responsible for the maintenance, development and review of the National Framework of Qualifications (NFQ).

See www.qqi.ie for more information.

All students should be aware of where the course they are studying is placed on the NFQ 'fan'. They should make sure that the course is recognised nationally and that it includes a recognised progression route. It is also useful for students to realise that there are a number of different agencies in Ireland currently working on consolidating recognised progression routes for a number of vocational areas, including early years;

and this process is ongoing as more and more pathways are validated and upgraded.

In 2011, all the Early Years FETAC Certificates were reviewed and changed to facilitate and streamline training nationwide. Before 2011, early years training was available from a number of different state training agencies. This was unsatisfactory as it meant that all students who were registered to train in childcare were doing different training, i.e. not every student was studying the same childcare modules. Thus, there was a need to standardise the childcare training sector.

The first step in professionalising the childcare sector was to set out a recognised training path; and there could be no recognised path if courses were not the same countrywide. To make a comparison with the Leaving Certificate, it is widely known that if you study honours English for the Leaving Certificate – whether you are studying in Cork, Dublin or Donegal – the course material covered is exactly the same. This is because there is a recognised, accredited curriculum for this subject.

The process of standardising training resulted in the development of new certificates for a number of vocational training areas. There are now full certificates available at Levels 4, 5 and 6, which will allow future students, in particular those who are returning to education after a long absence, an entrance into the certification arena. The new certificates all comprise eight modules in total, six of which are mandatory (i.e. all students must do these modules) and two electives (which are usually decided by the college).

Within the early years sector there has been for a number of years the development of profiles of staff who work within the sector. These profiles were originally developed to help set standards in the sector and also to help staff recognise and 'place' themselves within the recognised profiles and to then use this as another tool in the decision-making process on further training and progression in the sector. The following information and tables were taken from the discussion paper 'Developing the Workforce in the Early Childhood Care and Education Sector' (DES 2009) and can be used by students as an aid to career planning and selection.

OCCUPATIONAL PROFILES: SETTING STANDARDS

It is necessary for the future development of the childcare workforce in Ireland that education and training programmes equip practitioners with the essential skills, knowledge and competencies and promote the core values and dispositions necessary for high-quality practice. Occupational profiles provide the necessary benchmarks for the development of standards for education and training programmes. This section provides an overview of the development of occupational profiles for the ECCE sector in Ireland and looks at Frameworks of Qualifications in operation, both here and abroad.

Building occupational profiles

In 2002, the Department of Justice, Equality and Law Reform conducted an extensive consultation process to discover the scope and nature of occupational profiles in early childhood care and education in Ireland. This exercise culminated in the publication of *Quality Childcare and Lifelong Learning: Model Framework for Education, Training and Professional Development*. This publication identified a number of occupational profiles and associated skills/attributes depending on the role of the childcare practitioner. The roles range from Basic Practitioner to Expert Practitioner and are detailed below.

OCCUPATIONAL PROFILES

Occupational Profile	Intellectual Skills/Attributes	Processes	Accountability
Basic Practitioner	Elementary understanding of core knowledge areas. Ability to apply solutions to familiar problems. Ability to receive and pass on information.	Ability to carry out routine tasks. Basic competence in a range of clearly defined operations.	Directed activity under supervision. Reliance on external monitoring and quality control.
Intermediate Practitioner	Broad range of core knowledge with some depth. Ability to interpret and reflect on information. Well-developed range of practical skills.	Ability to carry out varied range of tasks in a limited range of different contexts.	Responsibility for own actions under direction. Some responsibility for quality of services within prescribed guidelines.
Experienced Practitioner	Broad range of core knowledge with greater depth. Ability to acquire specialist theoretical knowledge in one area. Ability to access, evaluate, compare and interpret information. Well-developed range of skills and ability to employ them in complex non-routine situations.	Ability to select from a broad range of skills appropriate to context. Present information to audience.	Operate with full autonomy with broad guidance/ evaluation. Responsibility for quality of services in accordance with specified standards. Limited responsibility for work of others.
Advanced Practitioner	In-depth understanding of comprehensive body of knowledge. Expertise in particular area of knowledge. Generate responses, demonstrating some innovation, to challenging situations. Analyse, evaluate and interpret a wide range of information.	Perform effectively in a wide range of contexts involving creative and non-routine activities. Use judgement in planning, selecting or presenting information, methods or resources.	Full autonomy and responsibility for own actions and those of others. Responsibility for meeting required quality standards.

| Expert Practitioner | Mastery of complex theoretical knowledge. Ability to critically evaluate knowledge, concepts and practice. Expertise in research, policy development. | Apply diagnostic and creative skills in a wide range of situations. Engage in planning, policy development and management. Engagement in research, publication and dissemination of knowledge and skills. | Complete autonomy in professional activities. Responsibility for achieving personal and group outcomes. Accountability for all decision making. |

Source: DJELR 2002.

MODEL FRAMEWORK OCCUPATIONAL PROFILES

Occupational Profile from the Model Framework	NFQ Level	Comment
Basic Practitioner	Level 4	This may need to equate to a major award or the best fit may be to a minor or special purpose award at that level.
Intermediate Practitioner	Level 5	This would generally equate to a major award (FETAC Level 5 Certificate) while it may also equate to a minor or a special purpose award.
Experienced Practitioner	Level 6	This would generally equate to a FETAC Advanced Certificate at Level 6.
Advanced Practitioner	Level 7/8	This would equate to at least an Ordinary Bachelor Degree.
Expert Practitioner	Level 8/9	This would equate to at least an Honours Bachelor Degree.

Source: DJELR 2002.

By using these guidelines students can see where they 'fit' in the profiles and then plan their progression route from there.

Levels 5 and 6: further training and progression

For most students who complete their FETAC Level 5 Early Childhood Care and Education (ECCE) Certificate and who are interested in further training, the next step would be to look at the FETAC Level 6 ECCE Certificate, which is available with a number of different training options. A number of institutions offer this training and most students will be able to find a training model that suits their current needs, whether full time, part time, module by module or distant/elearning provision.

As with the FETAC Level 5 ECCE Certificate, you need to complete eight modules in order to gain certification, six of which are mandatory and the other two electives, usually decided by the college. Apart from electing to continue on your learning journey there are a number of college options available to students should you decide to move straight from Level 5 to Level 7 (ordinary first degree) or Level 8 (honours first degree). Degree programmes in ECCE are also offered on a part-time and full-time basis.

Over the last five years or so the options for students to move from Level 5 to degree-level training have increased every year. A significant number of institutes of technology (ITs) offer a degree in early years care and education, as do a number of universities, private colleges and other training agencies around the country. Students can select a part-time or full-time option. More information on this topic can be found at www.qualifax.ie, the National Learners' Database.

> The National Learners' Database (www.qualifax.ie) holds up-to-date information about all courses on all subject areas in Ireland.

The same progression route applies to those students who are studying at Level 6 and, indeed, some colleges now offer credits to students who are entering at this level. Students should make individual enquiries about how this process works and where this option is available.

To apply for full-time college or university courses you need to apply through the Central Applications Office (CAO). You can do this online at www.cao.ie. You can apply using your FETAC results or as a mature student if you are over 23 years old. Applications to part-time degree-level ECCE courses are usually made direct to the college or university.

EMPLOYMENT

On completion of the FETAC Level 5 ECCE Certificate, students have a range of employment opportunities. Some of these opportunities are listed below, but this list is by no means exhaustive.

Play leader/assistant: all crèches and pre-schools

Qualification required: FETAC Level 5 ECCE Certificate.
The role would involve:

- working as part of a team, ensuring legislative guidelines are followed in daily activities
- running or helping to run a room in the ECCE service
- using your knowledge of Aistear and Síolta to design and implement programmes suitable for the age and capabilities of those children attending your room.

Room supervisor: all crèches and pre-schools

Qualification required: FETAC Level 5 ECCE Certificate.
This role is very similar to the play leader, except that in some instances the supervisors can have responsibility for the smooth running and operations of more than one room.

The job would involve:

▸ being responsible for staff (including setting rosters, break times, etc.)

▸ communicating with parents

▸ ensuring completion of all legislative requirements to include fire drills, compliance with health and safety regulations, child welfare and protection.

Crèche/pre-school manager

Qualification required: FETAC Level 6 ECCE Certificate.

You would have responsibility for running the whole service. The move from working directly with the children to a managerial position would usually indicate a shift into the more business-related aspect of the sector. Specific duties would include staffing, budgeting, administrative duties, enrolment, dealing with parents and any other issues that might arise. Some managers are still very hands-on with the children, but this is not the norm: most managers are responsible for ensuring that the service runs at capacity, and this in itself a full-time job.

Play assistant: national children's hospitals

Qualification required: FETAC Level 5 or 6 ECCE Certificate.

This role involves working with children who are in hospital for either long- or short-term stays. You would work both on the wards and in the play rooms, helping children play, using equipment if they are restricted in their movement. Play therapists are also attached to the hospitals, and play assistants work in a supportive role. The children's hospitals deal with all age groups from birth to 16 years old, and it would be expected that you would be capable of working with this diverse age group.

These positions are usually advertised on the specific hospital's website. They are also available through the Community Employment Schemes.

Screener: national maternity hospitals

Qualification required: FETAC Level 5 or 6 ECCE Certificate.

This role involves working with newborn babies and looking after them when the time comes for them to be vaccinated. It involves working alongside the doctors and nurses during the vaccination process.

Project support worker: voluntary childcare support agencies

Qualification required: FETAC Level 6 ECCE Certificate.

There are a number of different options in this type of work for students who are interested in working in this area, for example working with children at risk or in project support.

Working with children at risk

This usually involves working with families who are currently being supported by one of the agencies, and most commonly you would be based in their family home. This work can involve split shifts and weekend work, depending on the needs of the family you are working with. Duties include ensuring that children at risk have breakfast, get to school, complete their homework and are properly fed. After getting the children's breakfast, getting the children to school in the mornings and ensuring that they have whatever they need for the day, you would then be free (or perhaps working somewhere else) until the afternoon, when the children return from school. You would be expected to help with homework, ensure that the children are fed and that all their needs are met before finishing for the day.

Project support

This involves being employed within the community. A project support worker would usually be based in the community centre/hall and work with larger groups of children, following specific programmes and teaching specific life skills. The programmes and projects followed by the older children you work with are usually decided in collaboration with those attending the service, and following meetings and discussions. Programmes can range, for example, from an exhibition of work, which could be displayed locally, to helping decorate a run-down area in the community. These programmes can be run for a number of different reasons, but your main role would be working with 0–18-year-olds in a group-/club-type situation that would involve programme development.

These vacancies and various others are available on www.activelink.ie, which is regularly updated. The website also lists numerous volunteering opportunities: you could have the opportunity to volunteer with various countrywide agencies who work with children, and this could help you make decisions about your career and future opportunities.

As students progress up the training ladder, the number and choice of career options increases. During the work experience module you will have created a career action plan based on your study and career goals. Using the information in this chapter will inform your future choices.

Questions

1. What are the advantages and disadvantages of each type of employment opportunity listed in this chapter?

2. Identify study options for the following:

   ◆ Level 6

   ◆ Level 7

   ◆ Level 8

   ◆ Social care

   ◆ Healthcare

Using Technology to Find a Job

SOCIAL MEDIA AND ONLINE PROFILES

'Social media' is a general term that refers to the use of technology/online tools to communicate, collaborate, create content and share ideas. Many tools are available to communicate online, including Facebook, LinkedIn, Twitter, Blogger and more. For most people, social media is a way of having fun and communicating with friends and family; but more and more people are using social media tools to search for jobs. Using social media for job searching is a relatively new concept and requires some thought about your online profile.

Your 'online profile' is your online presence, or all the information about you on the Internet. You may be surprised to find information about yourself on the Internet, but most people have some online presence. The Internet can be either positive or negative: we have all heard about cyberbullying and its sometimes tragic effects; but if used correctly the Internet and its tools are very powerful and it is best not to ignore it. You are empowering yourself if you choose to educate yourself on how to use it. Childcare practitioners and parents need to understand how social media works and all the terminology that accompanies it. Although change can be a scary thing, once you begin to use social media you will be surprised at how much you can do with it. In this chapter, we will look at how to use social media as a job seeker.

LINKEDIN

In 2013, LinkedIn reached one million users in Ireland. Just imagine how many of those users might be related to the childcare sector. Now imagine being able to link to these practitioners and employers.

LinkedIn is a social media tool similar to Facebook but used by professionals. As with all social media, you start by setting up an account and creating a profile. LinkedIn can be used to describe your CV in more detail, and if you have a lot of work and life experience you can build a very detailed profile.

Since a CV should be no more than two pages in length, it really is a summary document of your experience and skills. As noted in Chapter 6, once you have created your CV it is a good idea to make it interactive by inserting hyperlinks to your online profile and more. As many CVs are now emailed, they are read on screen, so creating an interactive CV allows the reader to jump to your online profile for more information. Permitting the user to view your profile on LinkedIn can demonstrate that you are aware of the importance of building networks and communicating online. These alone are desirable skills. Inviting potential employers to discover more information about you demonstrates that you are a confident practitioner, even more so if the employer does not have the technical skills that you have used to promote yourself – because they will recognise that you have skills that could also be used to promote their business. Clients of potential employers may also view your profile online, thus being able to check your qualifications, your respectability and suitability for caring for and educating their children.

Your LinkedIn profile

Your profile should be honest and descriptive. Remember, an online profile is not a CV, but more a supplement to your CV, and it allows you to show your personality and interests. As with all social media, do not put information online that you would not wish anyone to see. If you are unsure how to get started, why not search for other childcare practitioners and look at their profiles? As with all social media tools, you can set the privacy of your profile, limiting who can view your information. You may choose to set this to a high privacy setting until you are comfortable with your profile, as building an interesting profile may take you some time.

Make your profile interactive by including the website links to your college and past employers. Include a photo in your profile so that people can see what you look like – this can enhance the connections you make on LinkedIn. Choose a photo that looks professional rather than a photo of you on holiday, for example. While on Facebook the people that are connected to you are called your **friends**, on LinkedIn they are known as **connections**. It is best practice only to connect to people you know or want to get to know in a professional context. You can search for people by name, just like Facebook, and send them a message that they receive by email and on LinkedIn. You are notified when they accept your invitation to connect. You can then view their profile and connections. By doing this, you are beginning the networking process.

> Think about who you could connect with when you first set up your LinkedIn account.

Endorsing skills and recommendations

One reason you should only connect with people you know or want to know is that they can **endorse** you for your skills. This is a powerful aspect of LinkedIn, as all your connections in effect become your referees. You can list your skills on LinkedIn, for example gardening, photography, baking, digital story creation, drawing, writing, dealing with challenging behaviour, special needs education, etc. Your connections can then see your skills and LinkedIn asks them to endorse your skills. You can see that over time your skills can be endorsed by many people. It is good **netiquette** to endorse your connections' skills when they have endorsed yours.

> Netiquette (Internet and etiquette) is the social norms and practices adhered to online.

This is similar to repaying a compliment in person or simply saying 'thank you for taking the time to endorse my skills'. Employers can see the list of skills for which you have been endorsed and are reassured that others agree with you. Employers can also see your connections and rate their importance; perhaps, for example, a college tutor or lecturer who has taken the time to praise your skills. Tutors and lecturers will not do this easily as they are concerned with their own reputation, so it is a good endorsement for you if they do.

Recommendations are different from endorsements. Recommendations involve one or more of your connections writing a recommendation on your LinkedIn profile, similar to a written reference. You could ask your referees to recommend you on LinkedIn.

> You could use the skills audit you conducted earlier in your course to decide which skills to add to your LinkedIn profile.

Interests

Another section that can enhance your profile is the section on interests. There is not much room on a CV to list your interests and hobbies, but on LinkedIn you can connect with groups that share your interests, companies that affect your practice or potential employers and influencers in the field of ECCE. If you follow **companies**, **influencers** and **groups** you will meet like-minded professionals.

> • **Influencers:** influential people, in different industry sectors, who write articles for LinkedIn that are designed to promote awareness of industry sectors, challenges, best practice, etc.
> • **Companies:** some companies have LinkedIn pages detailing their ethos, products and services.
> • **Groups:** professional groups set up to encourage knowledge sharing.

Joining LinkedIn groups can be a very supportive way of facing challenges in the workplace; you will find practitioners from all over the world discussing issues that you are facing. Using groups and influencers is an excellent way to get ideas for your own practice. You can join online conversations to share practice and find solutions to problems that you may face in your work placement and, eventually, your job. Joining groups demonstrates to potential employers that you are still involved in learning even if you are not yet working. Online communication and collaboration maintains and improves your knowledge. It is also important to be able to find the solution to challenges you are facing independently of your work placement supervisor or tutor/lecturer. You can search for groups on LinkedIn that can give advice on job seeking, CV tips, interview skills and much more. This is great evidence of independent learning. When you find helpful information in a group, you should recommend to your LinkedIn connections that the group is a valuable one.

Updating your status

Just as on Facebook, you can update your status on LinkedIn. Updating your status may include sharing **group** discussions you found valuable, for example a discussion on challenging behaviour, or sharing your own thoughts about legislation changes or commenting on challenges facing childcare practitioners in the workplace. You become more active and visible on LinkedIn by updating your status, thus attracting interest from other connections who may be beneficial to your job search. Reading newspapers, watching news and current affairs on television and posting your views and thoughts on newsworthy topics will demonstrate to a potential employer that you are interested in the sector and current challenges being faced.

Multimedia content

You can upload photos and videos to enhance your LinkedIn profile. You could include photos or videos of projects that children you care for have completed, photos of the room you supervise, etc. But remember: you must obtain parents' permission to use photos and videos of their children. If you do ask permission and they agree, always ask the parent to sign a release or consent form. If you have created any digital stories (podcasts) to accompany puppet shows, you can also include links to these on LinkedIn.

Searching for jobs

When you are looking for work, the most important aspect of LinkedIn is the **Jobs** section. You can search for jobs in different sectors nationally and worldwide. Companies will sometimes advertise only on LinkedIn, so you will see the job before others in the job market. You may also be able to see the information about the job poster/employer. Armed with this information, you can decide whether you would like to apply for the job. The advanced job search facility allows you to specify criteria such as location, company, country, experience level, job description and more.

TWITTER

Twitter is a microblogging social media tool. Microblogging means sending short messages or posts online. Twitter only allows the user to **tweet** messages of no more than 140 characters. (A tweet is a Twitter message.) Twitter users can tweet personal posts, but they can also share information and website links that  different sectors may find interesting. For example, teachers can use Twitter to share useful websites they have encountered. Just as on LinkedIn, users of Twitter can search for tweets about CV tips, career advice, etc.

> If you don't already have one, why not create a Twitter account now at www.twitter.com?

There are some strategies you can use to search for jobs on Twitter. As with LinkedIn, you can follow employment agencies' and potential employers' Twitter accounts to see any tweets about jobs.

> Think of some childcare-related organisations and search Twitter to see if they have an account.

If you have Twitter on your smartphone, you will receive a tweet the instant an employment agency tweets a job opportunity. This is very powerful in today's highly competitive job-seeking environment, as you can react instantly by tweeting your LinkedIn profile to the agency. In Chapter 6, we recommended that you email a copy of your CV and a cover letter to yourself so that you have immediate access to them should an opportunity come along. This is one such moment. You can email your CV directly to the agency in a matter of seconds.

Another strategy you can take advantage of is to tweet that you are looking for work. To ensure that your tweets are noticed and read by the right people, i.e. employment agencies and employers, you can target their Twitter account by including their Twitter account name in your tweet. You can also include links to your LinkedIn account so that an interested message receiver can view your profile to learn about you. You can use direct (private) messaging if you do not wish to make your tweets public. You may choose to use Twitter to look for casual work, such as babysitting, or tweet that you are a qualified childminder and are available for work.

> Putting the hashtag symbol (#) at the beginning of a word identifies messages on a specific topic, for example, #xfactor identifies tweets relating to the TV programme *The X Factor*.

Using hashtags to search for jobs is also a good strategy to use. Some hashtags to search for include *#jobsearch, #job, #jobfairy* and *#irishjobfairy*. The search will return a list of jobs on offer. The disadvantage is that the jobs are not specific to childcare: childcare jobs can be advertised this way, but you will need to look through all the tweets to identify them. A good tip is to take note of the date and time that the tweet was posted. If it is two months old, the vacancy has probably been filled.

FACEBOOK

In September 2013, research showed that Irish people use Facebook more than any other English-speaking country in the world (Weckler 2013). If you do not have a Facebook account, you are one of the very few! Facebook is used to communicate with friends and family, to share photos, videos, thoughts, jokes, retail offers, etc. Facebook pages can be created by organisations, businesses, community causes, charities and more.

Facebook may not be the best tool to discover jobs, but you can follow or 'Like' childcare facilities just in case they advertise. Organisations that you identified on Twitter may also have Facebook pages. Your Facebook friends may hear of available roles in childcare facilities and may share this with you on Facebook. Join childcare-related groups on Facebook, for example mother and baby groups or charity groups, and be active in expressing support and contributing to discussions. You can also place advertisements on Facebook to advertise that you are looking for work.

PROTECT YOUR REPUTATION

It is important to post tweets or Facebook statuses that are relevant to childcare. If you want to post personal tweets or put personal information on Facebook, it is probably best to create separate accounts. Keep one set of accounts for professional development and job searching and another for your personal life.

Always protect your profile by not posting information that a potential employer could take offence to. Do not comment on past employers in a negative way – this can lead to mistrust and negative views about you. Ask your friends to remove photos of you from their Facebook accounts that again could show you in a poor light.

BLOGGING

A blog – a **web log** – is a personal website used to express personal opinions, stories, experiences, etc. You may have heard of people blogging about food, recipes, local restaurant reviews or, indeed, of Hollywood bloggers writing about celebrity lifestyles. You can find blogs about everything from beauty to using technology to teach.

Visit www.blogger.com to set up an account. Search for blogs online – you might find some really good resources that will help you with your studies.

You may wonder how blogging could help you to get a job, but don't dismiss it yet. Earlier in the chapter, we considered LinkedIn and the different ways in which you can communicate your interests, skills and experiences to potential employers. Blogging is an excellent way to show potential employers that you have good written communication skills. You could, for example, showcase your knowledge about childcare by writing articles about any childcare issue or experience, such as how to deal with challenging behaviour. By posting your blog on your LinkedIn account you are inviting people to read your thoughts. We saw earlier that practitioners share ideas and discuss childcare-related topics in LinkedIn groups. Why not ask these practitioners what they think about your blogs? Don't be worried about receiving negative feedback: LinkedIn is for professionals who follow strict codes of conduct online. It is not like Facebook or Twitter, where people can sometimes be extremely nasty.

GOOGLE ALERTS

You can use Google Alerts to search for jobs too. If you set Google Alerts for childcare jobs, using your Google account, relevant alerts will be emailed to you on a day that you specify. You can also set Google Alerts for any childcare issues or

articles that appear on Google. You can use this information to inform your blogs or status updates on LinkedIn and Facebook. You can also set job alerts for companies you are interested in working for and you will receive emails instead of having to search for the jobs yourself.

MANAGING SOCIAL MEDIA ACCOUNTS

Managing the myriad of social media accounts can be tricky; if not done well, social media will be an ineffective way of job searching. If you are a beginner with social media and using the Internet to search for jobs, it may be best to start with just one account and master this account before moving on to others. LinkedIn would probably be the best tool to start with because jobs are advertised on this site, you can link with employers and you can expand your CV with lots of rich examples of your work.

It is possible to link LinkedIn and Facebook to Twitter accounts. This is handy as when you post to Facebook, Twitter also 'tweets' your post, saving you the trouble of posting the same message using two different social media accounts. Your Twitter feed (your tweets) can be displayed on your LinkedIn profile if you choose.

Some tools are available for managing multiple social media accounts; for example HootSuite (www.hootsuite.com)

allows you to manage several social media accounts through one application. You can add accounts and view posts and tweets, see who is following you, who is sending you messages, etc., all in one place. This is probably not for beginners, but it would be suitable for intermediate to advanced users of social media and the Internet.

BENEFITS OF USING SOCIAL MEDIA FOR JOB SEEKING

1. Provides a rich description of who you are, your skills and experience.
2. Supplements your CV.
3. Networking and making connections will improve your reputation.
4. Instant communication gives you an advantage when responding to job advertisements.
5. Mobile job searching (if you have the social media apps on your smartphone).
6. You can use the tools to create a personal brand for yourself and your skills by designing an effective profile.
7. You can save job advertisements on LinkedIn and Twitter to record jobs you have applied for and jobs you are interested in.
8. You can remain engaged with the profession and the job market by being active on social media groups.
9. You can use LinkedIn to research companies that you are interested in or that you are interviewing with.
10. Social media tools are free to use (although you can pay for a premium LinkedIn account to help you search for work).

CHALLENGES IN USING SOCIAL MEDIA FOR JOB SEEKING

1. You need to practise using social media tools to learn how to effectively use them for job searching.
2. You need intermediate to advanced IT skills to use them.
3. Employers you want to target may not have social media accounts and profiles.
4. There is a (small) risk of hacking and trolling.
5. It can be difficult to effectively manage many social media accounts.
6. You may sell yourself too high or too low for particular roles/jobs – it can be difficult to get the right balance of skills and experience in your profiles.
7. Some posts or tweets may not be noticed by employment agencies or employers – it is best to target them by using their account names or with private messaging.
8. Facebook is better suited to personal communications than professional communication and job seeking.
9. You cannot send private messages to companies or individuals that you are not connected to on LinkedIn.

10. You must consider legislation when publishing anything online: you cannot claim ideas or thoughts to be yours on a blog when someone else has written them first; be careful about using copyright images; be aware of data protection issues; and be aware of security.

11. Unless they are very specific, Twitter hashtags do not return specific childcare-related jobs in searches.

Questions and activities

1. Set up a LinkedIn account and use your skills audit to begin creating your profile. Create a plan of what you could use to enhance your profile and evidence your skills. If you cannot evidence some of your skills, consider whether you can use blogging to help.

2. Create a www.blogger.com account and write up a journal entry. Remember that your entry will appear online, so what should you do to ensure that children's identities are not revealed?

3. Set up a Twitter account and follow 10 organisations that are childcare related. Send your first tweet. Use the hashtag #WIC2014 and the account name @WIC2014 to show the authors of this book that you can use Twitter.

4. What are the advantages of using social media to search for jobs?

5. Compare the social media accounts discussed in this chapter. Which do you think is the best for job searching?

References and Resources

REFERENCES

AHECS (Association of Higher Education Careers Services) (n.d.) *Work Placement – A Best Practice Guide for Students* <http://www.hea.ie/sites/default/files/work-placement-a-best-practice-guide-for-students-ahecs-publication.pdf>.

APA (American Psychological Association) (1975) 'Edward L. Palmer', *American Psychologist* 30(1), January.

CECDE (Centre for Early Childhood Development and Education) (2006) *Síolta: the National Quality Framework for Early Childhood Education*. Dublin: CECDE.

DCYA (Department of Children and Youth Affairs) (2006) *Diversity and Equality Guidelines for Childcare Providers* <http://www.dcya.gov.ie/documents/childcare/diversity_and_equality.pdf> accessed 30 October 2013.

— (2011) *Children First: National Guidelines for the Protection and Welfare of Children* (revised). Dublin: Department of Children and Youth Affairs <http://www.dcya.gov.ie/documents/child_welfare_protection/Children_First_-_Key_messages.pdf>.

DES (Department of Education and Science) (2009) 'Developing the Workforce in the Early Childhood Care and Education Sector'. Dublin: DES.

DoHC (Department of Health and Children) (1996) *Child Care (Pre-School Services) Regulations 1996*. Dublin: Stationery Office.

— (2000) *Our Children – Their Lives: National Children's Strategy*. Dublin: Stationery Office.

— (2006) *National Childcare Strategy 2006–2010: A Guide for Parents*. Dublin: DoHC <http://www.dohc.ie/publications/pdf/en_childcare_parents.pdf?direct=1>.

DJLER (Department of Justice, Equality and Law Reform) (2002) *Quality Childcare and Lifelong Learning: Model Framework for Education, Training and Professional Development in the Early Childhood Care and Education Sector*. Dublin: Stationery Office.

Donohue, J. and Gaynor, F. (2011) *Education and Care in the Early Years*. Dublin: Gill & Macmillan.

Fade, S. (2005) 'Learning and Assessing through Reflection: A Practical Guide', available at <http://www.practicebasedlearning.org>.

Flood, Eilis (2013) *Child Development* (2nd edn). Dublin: Gill & Macmillan.

Flood, E. and Hardy, C. (2013) *Early Care and Education Practice.* Dublin: Gill & Macmillan.

Gladwell, Malcolm (2000) *The Tipping Point: How Little Things can Make a Big Difference.* USA: Little, Brown.

Kinsella, Joseph (2012) *Health, Safety and Welfare Law in Ireland.* Dublin: Gill & Macmillan.

Kolb, David A. (1983) *Experiential Learning: Experience as the Source of Learning and Development.* Englewood Cliffs, NJ: Prentice-Hall.

NCCA (National Council for Curriculum and Assessment) (2009a) *Aistear: The Early Childhood Curriculum Framework.* Dublin: NCCA.

— (2009b) *Aistear Toolkit,* available at <http://www.ncca.ie/en/Curriculum_and_Assessment/Early_Childhood_and_Primary_Education/Early_Childhood_Education/Aistear_Toolkit/>.

Richardson, Gillian and Maltby, Hendrika (1995) 'Reflection-on-practice: enhancing student learning', *Journal of Advanced Nursing 22* (2), 235–42.

Schön, Donald (1987) *Educating the Reflective Practitioner.* San Francisco, CA: Jossey-Bass.

UN (United Nations) (2010) Convention on the Rights of the Child. Dublin: Children's Rights Alliance <http://www.childrensrights.ie/sites/default/files/submissions_reports/files/UNCRCEnglish_0.pdf>.

UNESCO (United Nations Educational, Scientific and Cultural Organisation) (2000) *The Salamanca Statement and Framework for Action on Special Needs Education,* adopted by the World Conference on Special Needs Education: Access and Quality, Salamanca, Spain, 7–10 June 1994. UNESCO.

Wallace, Harold R. and Masters, L. Ann (2006) *Personality Development.* Australia: South-Western Cengage Learning.

Weckler, Adrian (2013) 'Irish are the Biggest Facebook Users in English-speaking World', *Irish Independent,* 18 September <www.independent.ie/business/technology/irish-are-the-biggest-facebook-users-in-englishspeaking-world-29587083.html>.

USEFUL WEBSITES

Active link: the online network for Irish non-profit organisations – www.activelink.ie

Apple in Education – www.apple.com/education/ipad/teaching-with-ipad/

Barnados – www.barnardos.ie

beSMART – www.besmart.ie

Burlington Early Childhood Center – http://burlingtonintegratedpreschool.blogspot. ie/2012/04/new-technology-in-burlington-early.html

Blogger – www.blogger.com

Careerjet – www.careerjet.ie

Central Applications Office (CAO) – www.cao.ie

Data Protection Commissioner – www.dataprotection.ie

Department of Children and Youth Affairs –www.dcya.gov.ie

Department of Education – www.education.ie

Early Childhood Ireland – www.earlychildhoodireland.ie

Education Posts – www.educationposts.ie

Equality Authority – www.equality.ie

Facebook – www.facebook.com

Food Safety Authority of Ireland – www.fsai.ie

Further Education and Training Awards Council (FETAC) – www.fetac.ie

Health and Safety Authority (HSA) – www.hsa.ie

Health Service Executive (HSE) – www.hse.ie

Hootsuite – www.hootsuite.com

Irish Congress of Trade Unions (ICTU) – www.ictu.ie

Irish Jobs – www.irishjobs.ie

Irish Statute Book – www.irishstatutebook.ie

Jobs Ireland – www.jobsireland.ie

LinkedIn – www.linkedin.com

Monster (jobs website) – www.monster.ie

National Council for Curriculum and Assessment – www.ncca.ie

National Framework of Qualifications (NFQ) – www.nfq.ie

Pobal – www.pobal.ie

Qualifax – www.qualifax.ie

Quality and Qualifications Ireland (QQI) – www.qqi.ie

Síolta – www.siolta.ie

Skype – www.skype.com

Twitter – www.twitter.com

UNESCO – www.unesco.org

Workplace Relations – www.employmentrights.ie